G000045478

QUIET MOMENTS for a MOTHER'S HEART

QUIET MOMENTS
for a MOTHER'S HEART

encouragement to warm
your heart and home

BETHANYHOUSE
MINNEAPOLIS, MINNESOTA

As a mother comforts her child,
so I'll comfort you.

—Isaiah 66:13 THE MESSAGE

CONTENTS

INTRODUCTION

Do not fear, for I am with you;
Do not anxiously look about you, for I am your God.
I will strengthen you, surely I will help you,
Surely I will uphold you with My righteous right hand.

Isaiah 41:10 NASB

At home or away, day or night, rain or shine—as a mom you are always available to meet the needs of your family with loving care. Yet where can you turn when you long for a moment of personal encouragement and understanding?

Turn to one of the meditations in *Quiet Moments for a Mother's Heart*. You will discover uplifting reflections and insights spoken uniquely to the heart of a mom. Each meditation provides an opportunity for the burdens and the tensions of the day to drift away as you enjoy a brief time of quiet solitude and communion with God.

You may browse through the meditation titles and choose each day the selection that addresses your present need, or you may prefer to simply read the meditations in the order they are printed. Either way, God will speak to your heart and restore your spirit during these quiet moments for mothers.

*If I were the mighty, roaring sea with waters
that surge and foam,*

*I'd know the hand that traced the shore and
set the boundaries of my home.*

*If I were a faraway glittering star ablaze in
the nighttime sky,*

*I'd know the hand that fashioned the heavens
and secured me proud and high.*

*If I were a mountain of jagged stone so tall I
towered o'er the earth,*

*I'd know the hand that carved my form and
determined its height and girth.*

*But I am one whom the Maker calls "child,"
and He is a Father to me.*

*So I know the hand that gently grasps mine
and gives me security.*

Melinda Mahand

*The LORD is good to those who depend on him,
to those who search for him. So it is good
to wait quietly for salvation from the LORD.*

Lamentations 3:25–26 NLT

LOVING EMBRACES

A Moment to Rest

As you pause from the activities of your day, let your mind and your body rest for a moment. Sink into the pillows of a soft chair or couch and feel the tension leave you. As you let relaxation wrap you in comfort, think about the people you have wrapped your arms around throughout the years—your newborn child those first precious weeks of life, your toddler after her first steps, a long-missed friend, or your husband at the end of a tough week.

> *Our great matters are little to God's infinite power, and our little matters are great to His Father's love.*
>
> Donald Grey Barnhouse

As you enjoy these memories, realize that your arms are not only the receivers of comfort and security, but they are the givers of these blessings as well. No one else can provide your children the assurance they find and the peace they experience when they are wrapped in your arms and comforted by your voice. Although your children may sometimes flex their tiny muscles to impress you, and although they may pretend to be fierce in games of make-believe, you know they would instantly run to the protective shelter of your arms if a real threat arose. They find comfort and strength in your arms.

In the same way, you find safety and peace in God's arms. He longs to hold you and give you the assurance you need to finish your tasks and meet the challenges of the day. Stop long enough to sense his loving embrace.

A Moment to Reflect

I have set the LORD always before me.
Because he is at my right hand, I will not be shaken.
Therefore my heart is glad and my tongue rejoices;
my body also will rest secure.

Psalm 16:8–9 NIV

God longs to be the protective arms and reassuring voice in your life. He waits for you to run to him when you need shelter, comfort, or strength. He will gently hold you in his care and speak the words your heart so desperately needs to hear: You are safe, my child. Rest here in my arms.

These moments of rest offer a quiet opportunity for you to talk to God. He cares deeply about the tasks and concerns that have overwhelmed your heart today. He will restore your inner being as you linger in the safety of his presence and listen to the reassuring words he whispers to your heart.

The thunder rolled; the storm clouds blew.
Yet my child slept the whole night through.
Securely tucked within my arm,
She knew that she was safe from harm.
Lord, help me learn to trust in You
When storm clouds blow in my life, too.
Hold me close within Your care,
And let me find true shelter there.

Melinda Mahand

A Moment to Refresh

*When you keep
your face turned
toward God, He
will give you rest
from worry
and fear.*

Diane Noble

*God has promised
to keep his people,
and he will keep
his promise.*

Charles Haddon
Spurgeon

*The everlasting God is your place of safety,
and his arms will hold you up forever.*

Deuteronomy 33:27 NCV

*Powerful is your arm! Strong is your hand!
Your right hand is lifted high in glorious
strength. Righteousness and justice are
the foundation of your throne. Unfailing
love and truth walk before you as
attendants. Happy are those who hear
the joyful call to worship, for they
will walk in the light of your
presence, LORD.*

Psalm 89:13–15 NLT

*God's Spirit doesn't make us slaves who are
afraid of him. Instead, we become his children
and call him our Father. God's Spirit makes us
sure that we are his children. His Spirit lets us
know that together with Christ we will be given
what God has promised. We will also share
in the glory of Christ, because we
have suffered with him.*

Romans 8:15–17 CEV

FOCUS ON GOD

A Moment to Rest

Meditative prayer offers a great rest for your heart. It soothes and comforts you as you take a moment to set aside your personal concerns and rest quietly in the presence of God.

Morning, noon, or night—the time of day you choose to pray doesn't matter. The place where you pray doesn't matter much either. As a mother juggling the busyness of children's needs, household chores, work responsibilities, and family activities, finding a quiet moment often seems impossible. But there are times during each day—in a favorite chair, on the porch swing, at the breakfast table, or at your desk—when you can close your eyes and focus your attention completely on God. Actively consider the majesty of the earth he has created. As the images of snowcapped mountains, ocean breakers, brilliant sunsets, delicate seashells, and brightly blossoming flowers come to mind, thank God for each image.

> *Prayer is ordained to this end that we should confess our needs to God, and bare our hearts to him, as children lay their troubles in full confidence before their parents.*
>
> John Calvin

As you consider the wonders of God's greatness, release yourself into his care. Consciously remind yourself that the God who keeps the sun, moon, and stars moving in their orbits, the God who created the earth and all its wonders, is more than able to guard and keep you.

Come away from your prayerful minutes strengthened and rested.

A Moment to Reflect

The LORD directs the steps of the godly.
He delights in every detail of their lives.
Though they stumble, they will never fall,
for the LORD holds them by the hand.

Psalm 37:23–24 NLT

When you were a child, you didn't worry about the rent or taxes or anything else outside the realm of your young world. Your parents took care of all that. You can't return to the carefree days of childhood, but you can put your hand in God's hand and trust him to help you face your days with joy and contentment. He wants you to express your needs, your desires, your frustrations and allow him to give you his strength, help, and hope.

If you are feeling overwhelmed by the demands of your hectic life, God wants you to know that he is ready to come alongside and help you sort through the clutter. Together you can achieve a balanced lifestyle that includes rest and relaxation.

There is an hour of calm relief
From every throbbing care;
'Tis when before a throne of grace,
I kneel in secret prayer,
When one by one, like threads of gold,
The hues of twilight fall,
Oh, sweet communion with my God,
My Saviour and my all!

Fanny J. Crosby

Let us . . . approach the throne of grace with boldness, so that we may receive mercy and find grace to help in time of need.

Hebrews 4:16 NRSV

Don't worry about anything, but in all your prayers ask God for what you need, always asking him with a thankful heart. And God's peace, which is far beyond human understanding, will keep your hearts and minds safe in union with Christ Jesus.

Philippians 4:6–7 GNT

I ask for your help, LORD God, and you will keep me safe. Morning, noon, and night you hear my concerns and my complaints.

Psalm 55:16–17 CEV

I look up to the mountains — does my help come from there? My help comes from the LORD, who made heaven and earth! . . . The LORD keeps you from all harm and watches over your life. The LORD keeps watch over you as you come and go, both now and forever.

Psalm 121:1–2, 7–8 NLT

I cry aloud to the LORD; I lift up my voice to the LORD for mercy. I pour out my complaint before him; before him I tell my trouble. When my spirit grows faint within me, it is you who know my way.

Psalm 142:1–3 NIV

Is not prayer precisely of itself peace, silence, strength, since it is a way of being with God?

Jacques Illul

Prayer serves as an edge and border to preserve the web of life from unraveling.

Robert Hall

Shaped by His Hand

A Moment to Rest

Like people and snowflakes, every tree is unique. Each is truly a one-of-a-kind creation, with a shape and design all its own. Perhaps that's why a tree never fails to inspire a sense of wonder when you stop to take a closer look.

Poems are made by fools like me, but only God can make a tree.

Joyce Kilmer

In the midst of your busy day, take time out to ponder the magnificence of a tree that lives and grows near you. Do your children have a favorite climbing tree? Or is there a tree that shades your favorite thinking spot?

Stop and really look at that tree. Slowly run your hand along its trunk. Is the bark smooth and a little sticky, made up of hard lumpy squares, or something in between? Take one of its leaves and trace its lines and ridges with your fingertips. Step back and gaze up into the branches, noting the way they have been shaped and turned by the wind and rain. Imagine the roots burrowing underground, providing stability, strength, and nourishment.

As you do this, consider the fact that you are God's unique creation. Like the tree, you are one of a kind, molded and shaped by his hand. Let that understanding lift and refresh your spirit. Then open your heart and whisper a greeting to him, the Creator of all things.

A Moment to Reflect

I am like a green olive tree in the house of God;
I trust in the mercy of God forever and ever.

Psalm 52:8 NKJV

God created all the wonders we see in the natural world. When he was finished, he looked it over and said that it was good. Then he created man and woman. God created human beings, unlike trees and other elements of his creation, in his very own image. He invested in each person a singular combination of godlikeness.

If your busy lifestyle has left you feeling lost in the crowd, slow down for a few quiet moments to consider your own uniqueness. Stretch your arms out toward the sky and imagine your roots going deep into God's very being—drinking in nourishment for your spirit. As Paul wrote in the book of Ephesians: "Your roots will grow down into God's love and keep you strong" (3:17 NLT).

Tossed on a windy sea the great oak surrenders its last brittle
browning leaves to the silent ground below—still she
stands—arms upraised—to sing the psalm of
seasons, of God's eternal praise.

Tara Afriat

You will go out in joy and be led forth in peace; the
mountains and hills will burst into song before you,
and all the trees of the field will clap their hands.

Isaiah 55:12 NIV

A Moment to Refresh

No town can fail of beauty, though its walks were gutters and its houses hovels, if venerable trees make magnificent colonnades along its street.

Henry Ward Beecher

A woodland in full color is awesome as a forest fire, in magnitude at least; but a single tree is like a dancing tongue of flame to warm the heart.

Hal Borland

Happy are those who . . . find joy in obeying the Law of the LORD, and they study it day and night. They are like trees that grow beside a stream, that bear fruit at the right time, and whose leaves do not dry up. They succeed in everything they do.

Psalm 1:1–3 GNT

They will be called oaks of righteousness, The planting of the LORD, that He may be glorified.

Isaiah 61:3 NASB

The fruit of the righteous is a tree of life.

Proverbs 11:30 NKJV

To him who overcomes, I will grant to eat of the tree of life which is in the Paradise of God.

Revelation 2:7 NASB

The righteous shall flourish like a palm tree, He shall grow like a cedar in Lebanon.

Psalm 92:12 NKJV

WAITING . . . PATIENTLY?

A Moment to Rest

Today you have spent most of your time taking care of everyone else—making sure lunches were packed, the kids arrived at school on time, your work deadlines were met, the errands were run . . . and the list goes on. Now, give a few moments back to yourself. Go to your favorite comfortable chair or sunlit table. Wait for your mind to stop racing and your pulse to slow down. Let this quiet moment be a gift of restoration to your inner self.

> *Speaking the truth in love, we are to grow up in all aspects into Him who is the head, even Christ.*
>
> Ephesians 4:15
> NASB

Unfortunately, restoration is not the usual result of waiting in today's society. We tend to grow fidgety if we stand in a checkout line or sit in a doctor's office for even a few minutes. In our attempt to avoid waiting, we master everything from instant oatmeal to instant messages. We expect our food fast and our packages overnight. Simply put, we consider waiting to be a waste of time.

Yet God's attitude toward waiting is dramatically different from ours, for God willingly waits with patience and gentleness toward us. Just as our children were not born fully mature adults, neither were we instantly mature when we first trusted God. In fact, we were mere "infants in Christ" (1 Corinthians 3:1 NIV). So God—our parent—patiently waits and watches with expectation for signs of growth in us—his children.

A Moment to Reflect

Continue to grow in the grace and knowledge
of our Lord and Savior Jesus Christ. To him
be the glory, now and forever! Amen.

2 Peter 3:18 GNT

Without anxiety, without discouragement, ask God to guide your heart as you consider your growth in Christ thus far. How far down the road to maturity have you walked?

Too often when we consider spiritual growth, we feel like complete failures, and as a result of those feelings, we give up. So today, neither focus on past failures, except to ask forgiveness for them, nor focus on present successes, except to praise God for them. Focus instead on where God wants you to be tomorrow and ask him the steps to take to get there. As you read his Word and talk with him, his Spirit will guide you. Remember always that he is patiently waiting for you to learn the way.

Gradual growth in grace, growth in knowledge, growth in
faith, growth in love, growth in holiness, growth in humility,
growth in spiritual-mindedness —all this I see clearly taught
and urged in Scripture, and clearly exemplified in the lives of
many of God's saints. But sudden, instantaneous leaps from
conversion to consecration I fail to see in the Bible.

J. C. Ryle

You give me your shield of victory, and your right hand
sustains me; you stoop down to make me great.

Psalm 18:35 NIV

*Like newborn babies, crave pure spiritual
milk, so that by it you may grow up in
your salvation, now that you have
tasted that the Lord is good.*

1 Peter 2:2–3 NIV

*You, dear friends, must build each other up in
your most holy faith, pray in the power of the
Holy Spirit, and await the mercy of our
Lord Jesus Christ, who will bring you
eternal life. In this way, you will
keep yourselves safe in God's love.*

Jude 20–21 NLT

*My beloved, just as you have always obeyed,
not as in my presence only, but now much
more in my absence, work out your
salvation with fear and trembling; for it
is God who is at work in you, both to
will and to work for His good pleasure.*

Philippians 2:12–13 NASB

*Do not ignore this one fact, beloved, that with
the Lord one day is like a thousand years, and
a thousand years are like one day. The Lord is
not slow about his promise, as some think of
slowness, but is patient with you, not wanting
any to perish, but all to come to repentance.*

2 Peter 3:8–9 NRSV

*Our ground of
hope is that God
does not weary
of mankind.*

Ralph W. Sockman

*Happy is he who
makes daily
progress and who
considers not
what he did
yesterday but
what advance he
can make today.*

Jerome

LIVING REFLECTIONS

A Moment to Rest

Are you ready for a break today? Stop and reflect on the woman who helped mold who you are, how you think, what you believe, and how you behave. She may be your mother, or she may be another woman in your life who nurtured and encouraged you.

Be imitators of God, therefore, as dearly loved children.

Ephesians 5:1
NIV

Her influence was deeply embedded in your heart when you were just a child. She influenced your character, your values, your thoughts, your beliefs, and your behaviors. In the same way, you are helping to mold and shape the people your children will become.

Although you are now an adult, your mother's influence sometimes bubbles unexpectedly to the surface, and you suddenly recognize her reflection in your words or actions. Or you may have seen your own reflection in what your child says and does. Perhaps you chuckled as you recognized the similarities. Perhaps you even secretly felt grateful to see the family resemblance.

Because you are a dearly loved child of God, you reflect his influence in your life. His being has been deeply embedded in your heart. He now molds who you are, how you think, what you believe, and how you behave. As you grow to reflect more and more of him, he gives you the privilege of being his living reflection to the world. You are actually invited to imitate him!

A Moment to Reflect

My dear friend, do not imitate what is bad, but imitate what is good. Whoever does good belongs to God.

3 John 11 GNT

When your life begins to reflect God's influence, you enjoy the benefits of belonging to him and giving him pleasure. Yet equally as important is what God's reflection offers to the world. As his child, you have an amazing opportunity to let people glimpse what God is like. Your life becomes a physical demonstration of God's love and power to those who do not know him. He uses your example and your life to draw people to him.

Thank God today for this amazing privilege. Commit to grow more in his image each day. Imagine how pleased he will be when his influence comes bubbling to the surface and you begin to imitate him. Think how he will delight to see the family resemblance.

I would be true, for there are those who trust me;
I would be pure, for there are those who care;
I would be strong, for there is much to suffer;
I would be brave, for there is much to dare.
I would be prayerful, through each busy moment;
I would be constantly in touch with God.
I would be tuned to hear His slightest whisper;
I would have faith to keep the path Christ trod.

Howard Al Walter

A Moment to Refresh

You are Light in the Lord; walk as children of Light (for the fruit of the Light consists in all goodness and righteousness and truth), trying to learn what is pleasing to the Lord.

Ephesians 5:8–10 NASB

Remember your leaders who taught you the word of God. Think of all the good that has come from their lives, and follow the example of their faith.

Hebrews 13:7 NLT

God . . . has chosen you, because our gospel came to you not simply with words, but also with power, with the Holy Spirit and with deep conviction. You know how we lived among you for your sake. You became imitators of us and of the Lord; in spite of severe suffering, you welcomed the message with the joy given by the Holy Spirit. And so you became a model to all the believers.

1 Thessalonians 1:4–7 NIV

May our Lord Jesus Christ himself and God our Father, who loved us and in his grace gave us unfailing courage and a firm hope, encourage you and strengthen you to always do and say what is good.

2 Thessalonians 2:16–17 GNT

Where one reads the Bible, a hundred read you and me.

Dwight L. Moody

The Christian is called to be the partner of God in the conversion of men.

William Barclay

GOOD THINGS

A Moment to Rest

Stretch out, gaze into the sky, and consider eternity with God. What do you think heaven will be like? What do you look forward to about being there? Most of us anticipate heaven, but we don't know a lot about it. We know that it's full of God's goodness and blessings. But you don't have to wait for heaven. God wants you to experience his goodness and blessings right now.

When we are focused on life's troubles, we sometimes have a hard time recognizing that God wants good things for us. We are often like the child who chases his ball into the street. The child sees only his ball and not the approaching car. When his mother grabs him out of the street, the child recognizes only that his toy has been lost, not that his life wasn't.

The LORD God is a sun and shield; The LORD gives grace and glory; No good thing does He withhold from those who walk uprightly.

Psalm 84:11 NASB

Because the child is focused on mourning his loss, he cannot appreciate being secure in his mother's arms.

Sometimes, everything seems to be going wrong: The kids are experiencing a difficult phase, you're having financial trouble, you and your spouse can't seem to get along, someone you love has been diagnosed with cancer. . . . The list of human struggles is endless. But no matter what you face, God wants and plans good things for you. You can trust him. You are his child.

A Moment to Reflect

Oh, how great is Your goodness,
Which You have laid up for those who fear You,
Which You have prepared for those who trust in You.

Psalm 31:19 NKJV

Have you experienced the loss of things precious to you? Has that loss caused you to lose sight of God's goodness and blessing? Begin today to retrain the focus of your heart so that you can recognize God's hand of goodness and blessing in your life.

What good thing has God recently sent your way? What new opportunity has he given? In what area has he blessed you with a second chance? Through whom has he worked to bring you help or encouragement? Recognize these gifts as being from the hand of God. Thank him for them individually and specifically. Then begin to watch for his goodness and blessing each day—because God truly does not withhold good from his children.

God often takes a course for accomplishing His purposes
directly contrary to what our narrow views would prescribe.
He brings a death upon our feelings, wishes, and prospects
when He is about to give us the desire of our hearts.

John Newton

Let them give thanks to the LORD for his unfailing love and
his wonderful deeds for men, for he satisfies the thirsty
and fills the hungry with good things.

Psalm 107:8–9 NIV

[Jesus said,] "Is there anyone among you who, if your child asks for bread, will give a stone? Or if the child asks for a fish, will give a snake? If you then, who are evil, know how to give good gifts to your children, how much more will your Father in heaven give good things to those who ask him!"

Matthew 7:9–11 NRSV

The LORD sustains all who fall
And raises up all who are bowed down.
The eyes of all look to You,
And You give them their food in due time.
You open Your hand
And satisfy the desire of every living thing.
The LORD is righteous in all His ways
And kind in all His deeds.

Psalm 145:14–17 NASB

God is able to make all grace abound to you, so that in all things at all times, having all that you need, you will abound in every good work. As it is written: "He has scattered abroad his gifts to the poor; his righteousness endures forever."

2 Corinthians 9:8–9 NIV

Those blessings are sweetest that are won with prayer and worn with thanks.

Thomas Goodwin

What kind of God are You, who does not make my dreams come true, but does things more impossible than even I can dream?

Melinda Mahand

INTO THE WORLD OF WORDS

A Moment to Rest

Nothing melts away stress like a good book. Whether you want to be inspired, instructed, or simply entertained, a book can lift you up and away from the cares of your busy day and take you into a world of beauty and adventure.

Read to refill the wells of inspiration.

Harold J. Ockenga

But where does a busy mother like you find the time to slip away into the world of words? If you have fifteen minutes, then fifteen minutes is all you need. Don't worry about being able to finish a whole book or even a chapter in one sitting. Pick up your book and read as much as time allows. It's okay if it takes weeks or even months to finish.

The type of reading you choose is completely up to you as well. You may prefer the escape provided by a good novel. You may enjoy the inspiration of a beautiful gift book. Perhaps you are drawn to the enrichment offered by nonfiction. Whatever your tastes, choose something that captures your interest and inspires you.

The great thing about reading is that you can do it almost anywhere: in the car while you're waiting to pick up your children, in the doctor's office as you wait to be seen, at your desk during a work break. Wherever you choose, a quiet moment to reenergize awaits you.

A Moment to Reflect

*Gracious speech is like clover honey—good taste
to the soul, quick energy for the body.*

Proverbs 16:24 THE MESSAGE

When you need a spurt of inspiration or a nudge of creativity, stop for a few minutes and give yourself a book break. Every mom needs a few quiet moments in the world of words.

As you make your reading selection, don't forget the most captivating book of all time—the Bible. Often called "the Good Book," the Bible contains fuel for the imagination, directions for living, power for changing things.

You know how children love to snuggle in your lap and listen to you read a good book. They enjoy the magic of the words and the joy of being close to you. You can experience that same kind of closeness with God as you read the Bible. God's words will resonate within your heart, filling your being with hope and encouragement, wonder and praise.

*And nature, the old nurse, took
The child upon her knee,
Saying, "Here is a story book
My father hath writ for thee.
Come wander with me," she said,
"In regions yet untrod
And read what is still unread
In the manuscripts of God."*

Henry Wadsworth Longfellow

A Moment to Refresh

While thought exists, words are alive and literature becomes an escape, not from, but into living.

Cyril Connolly

A book is like a garden carried in the pocket.

Ancient Proverb

My eyes are awake through the night watches,
That I may meditate on Your word.

Psalm 119:148 NKJV

The sayings of the wise are like the sharp sticks that shepherds use to guide sheep, and collected proverbs are as lasting as firmly driven nails. They have been given by God, the one Shepherd of us all.

Ecclesiastes 12:11 GNT

Happy is the one who reads this book, and happy are those who listen to the words of this prophetic message and obey what is written in this book! For the time is near when all these things will happen.

Revelation 1:3 GNT

A wise person gets known for insight; gracious words add to one's reputation.

Proverbs 16:21 THE MESSAGE

The Holy Scriptures . . . are able to make you wise for salvation through faith which is in Christ Jesus.

2 Timothy 3:15 NKJV

WALKING FOR YOUR BODY, MIND, AND SPIRIT

A Moment to Rest

Walking—we park close in to avoid it. We look at the "to-do" list and decide there's no time for it. We think about everything the kids have going on and decide there's just no way to fit walking into the schedule. Yet there are few better ways to calm your emotions and rest your mind than a good, brisk walk. Take it slow at first, and head out with no particular destination in mind. Walk for the simple joy of it.

> *Two legs with which to walk about on God's green earth, what greater store of blessing could be imagined?*
>
> Roberta S. Cully

As you walk along, focus on the sensation of your blood coursing through your veins—proof positive that you're alive. Lift your head and thank God for your life. Notice your muscles as they flex in your arms and legs. Lift your head and thank God for your strength. Feel the warmth in your face—a sign that your body is responding as it should. Lift your head and thank God for your health.

Adam walked with God in the cool of the evening, but the time of day wasn't what made that activity so special. It was the interaction enjoyed by Creator and created. As you walk, take advantage of the time to fellowship with your Creator. Tell him you're glad to be alive. Walk until you feel invigorated in your body and spirit.

A Moment to Reflect

You show me the path of life. In your presence
there is fullness of joy; in your right
hand are pleasures forevermore.

Psalm 16:11 NRSV

When you exercise and care for your body, you are ensuring
a safe and sturdy environment in which your spirit can grow
and flourish. Walking is one of the very best ways to keep
your body in shape.

For many busy mothers, it's hard to find a space in the day
to exercise, so ask your family to help you create a time for
walking. Walking is most beneficial when it's done on a regular basis. Start out with twenty or thirty minutes three times
a week. If walking is a new activity for you, resist the urge to
walk too far too fast. Over time, your body will adjust to the
exertion. Your strength and stamina will increase, your muscles will lose the ache, and your inner self will shout for the
joy of walking with God.

Walk quietly—and know that He is God. When evening
shadows lie against the hill—in the hush of twilight,
when the world is still. And the balm of peace
soothes every ill—walk quietly.

Author Unknown

You have delivered me from death and my feet from
stumbling, that I may walk before God in the light of life.

Psalm 56:13 NIV

Many nations will come and say, "Come and let us go up to the mountain of the LORD And to the house of the God of Jacob, That He may teach us about His ways And that we may walk in His paths."

Micah 4:2 NASB

"I am the light of the world," [Jesus] said. "Whoever follows me will have the light of life and will never walk in darkness."

John 8:12 GNT

He who says, "I know Him," and does not keep His commandments, is a liar, and the truth is not in him. But whoever keeps His word, truly the love of God is perfected in him. By this we know that we are in Him. He who says he abides in Him ought himself also to walk just as He walked.

1 John 2:4–6 NKJV

I will teach you wisdom's ways and lead you in straight paths. When you walk, you won't be held back; when you run, you won't stumble.

Proverbs 4:11–12 NLT

Take God for your bridegroom and friend, and walk with him continually; and you will not sin and will learn to love, and the things you must do will work out prosperously for you.

John of the Cross

We do not walk to God with the feet of our body, nor would wings, if we had them, carry us to Him, but we go to Him, by the affections of our soul.

Augustine of Hippo

FEET IN THE AIR

A Moment to Rest

For a busy mom, a few minutes of doing nothing can be as delicious as ice cream on a hot summer day. "Doing nothing" carries with it a sense of indulgence, of unexpected delight. And what says "doing nothing" better than sitting back and putting your feet up?

Nothing is a waste of time if you use the experience wisely.

Rodin

The truth is, those moments aren't indulgent at all. They provide a needed opportunity to reenergize both your body and your spirit. Putting your feet up is a good way to safeguard those brief times of rest and avoid the inclination to jump up and do something when the thought strikes you.

Find your favorite spot to kick back—wherever that may be—lose the shoes, wiggle your toes, and put your feet in the air. Close your eyes and let your mind drift away. Imagine yourself running barefoot through a meadow filled with soft green grass and wild flowers. Feel the grass tickling your toes and sliding warm and soft beneath the soles of your feet. Or imagine yourself running along the beach, the sand squishing up between your toes and the cool water splashing up around your ankles. It's a vacation you can't afford to miss.

A Moment to Reflect

My soul, wait in silence for God only,
For my hope is from Him.
He only is my rock and my salvation,
My stronghold; I shall not be shaken.
On God my salvation and my glory rest;
The rock of my strength, my refuge is in God.

Psalm 62:5–7 NASB

Most of us live life at a frenetic pace. Seldom do we have the opportunity to simply put our feet in the air. We often feel guilty if we *do* take a moment to kick back. But the reality is that humans—moms in particular—need rest, a chance to pull away from life's demands, and regroup. God himself rested after creation. He established a day of rest for his people. And Jesus understood his personal need to pull away from the crowds to reenergize.

Don't let guilt and your long to-do list keep you from enjoying what God intended—times here and there when all you need to do is put your feet up.

In the midst of my harried day when I seem farthest from
myself a moment comes to me and beckons, "Let us fly
away." Shutting out the din of the never-ending to-do,
I close my eyes and begin to wander in thoughts
sublime, and gather flowers in my mind.

Tara Afriat

❦

I will lie down and sleep in peace, for you alone,
O LORD, make me dwell in safety.

Psalm 4:8 NIV

A Moment to Refresh

Work is not always required of a man. There is such a thing as sacred idleness, the cultivation of which is now fearfully neglected.

George MacDonald

One cannot rest except after steady practice.

George Ade

*The LORD will give strength to His people;
The LORD will bless His people with peace.*

Psalm 29:11 NKJV

Those who live in the shelter of the Most High will find rest in the shadow of the Almighty.

Psalm 91:1 NLT

So many people were coming and going that Jesus and the apostles did not even have a chance to eat. Then Jesus said, "Let's go to a place where we can be alone and get some rest."

Mark 6:31 CEV

[The Lord] said, "My presence will go with you, and I will give you rest."

Exodus 33:14 NRSV

Let my soul be at rest again, for the LORD has been good to me.

Psalm 116:7 NLT

This is what the Sovereign LORD, the Holy One of Israel, says: "In repentance and rest is your salvation, in quietness and trust is your strength."

Isaiah 30:15 NIV

No Need to Worry

A Moment to Rest

Give yourself a few minutes to lean back and take several long, slow, deep breaths. As you exhale, allow the worries of the day to leave your mind.

Kim is a middle-aged mom who sometimes discovers a new worry her heart needs to let go of. During these times, she thinks of when her daughter was a baby. At six months old, Jenna began drinking from a bottle. So each night Kim would prepare a bottle for Jenna's early morning feeding and place it in the refrigerator. Then when a hungry cry rang out in the wee morning hours, all Kim had to do was heat the bottle.

> *Worry has an active imagination.*
>
> D. Martin Lloyd-Jones

Kim's heart would have broken if she had thought that Jenna spent one moment of the night worrying about whether there would be any milk for her the next morning. Kim would also have been hurt if she had thought that Jenna spent her nights plotting foolish and unnecessary schemes to get her needs met. As a young mother, Kim had known what Jenna's needs were and had been prepared to fulfill them. Kim had been ready to respond at the sound of her baby's cry.

Jenna had no reason to worry, no reason to fear. She could rest securely in the assurance that her needs would be filled. All she had to do was ask.

A Moment to Reflect

Don't worry about anything; instead, pray about every-
thing. Tell God what you need, and thank him for all he
has done. Then you will experience God's peace, which
exceeds anything we can understand. His peace will guard
your hearts and minds as you live in Christ Jesus.

Philippians 4:6–7 NLT

God knows you as intimately as a parent knows a child. Your needs do not surprise or intimidate him any more than a baby's need for milk surprises or intimidates a mother. God knows every one of your needs and is prepared to fulfill them before you even ask. Anxious days and sleepless nights are unnecessary—and what is more, they break God's heart.

Talk to God about the things that concern you this day, and seek his provision. Meet God in prayer and find your every need fulfilled. Trust that he will always be the loving parent who responds to your heartfelt needs.

When your worries seem to be many,
and your friends seem to be few,
When you're looking for something that's faithful,
When you're looking for someone who's true,
In the stillness of the nighttime or the pressing of the day,
Turn your anxious thoughts toward the heavens,
And impel your heart to pray.
For your God is always nearby;
He will come at the sound of your cry.

Melinda Mahand

A Moment to Refresh

Do not worry, saying, "What shall we eat?" or "What shall we drink?" or "What shall we wear?" For . . . your heavenly Father knows that you need them. But seek first his kingdom and his righteousness, and all these things will be given to you as well.

Matthew 6:31–33 NIV

Give ear to my words, O LORD,
Consider my meditation.
Give heed to the voice of my cry,
My King and my God,
For to You I will pray.
My voice You shall hear in
the morning, O LORD;
In the morning I will direct it to You,
And I will look up.

Psalm 5:1–3 NKJV

Which of you by worrying can add a single hour to his life's span? If then you cannot do even a very little thing, why do you worry about other matters?

Luke 12:25–26 NASB

Be confident, my heart, because the LORD has been good to me.

Psalm 116:7 GNT

Anxiety does not empty tomorrow of its sorrow; but only empties today of its strength.

Charles Haddon Spurgeon

Stop thinking about your difficulties, whatever they are, and start thinking about God instead.

Emmet Fox

HIDING IN THE FORTRESS

A Moment to Rest

Where is your favorite place to take a break, to hide for a few brief quiet moments from the demands of the day? Go there now. Enjoy the sanctuary this place offers your body and your mind.

The contentment you feel at having your own special place to hide from the world begins at a young age. How often has your child come to you for refuge, curled in your lap, nestled in your arms, or snuggled by your side?

You are my hiding place and my shield; I hope in Your word.

Psalm 119:114
NKJV

A relationship with someone who protects you, someone who makes you feel safe, someone in whose presence you can hide is a blessing nothing else in life can replace. Your inner being craves such security. Thus God may have blessed you with a parent, spouse, or friend through whom he works to help fulfill that need.

Yet discovering that another human being cannot completely fulfill your need for security does not take long. As a mom, you recognize that the battles of life loom large, the pain of losing is deep, and the aftereffects of the assault are long lasting. So today God offers you a hiding place, a fortress of refuge. He is your shelter, your rock, your place of safety in all the battles of life.

A Moment to Reflect

You are my strength; I wait for you to rescue me,
for you, O God, are my fortress.

Psalm 59:9 NLT

Historically, the fortress was not only a place where people were safe, but it was also a place where provisions were stored. Food and water, weaponry, and medical supplies were all housed within its walls.

Likewise, God not only offers you a place of security, but he also offers a place of provision.

In him you will discover nourishment and the strength life requires, weaponry for the battles life entails, and healing for the wounds life inflicts. Remember too that a fortress was almost always built around a town. It was not simply a place for retreat when threats loomed; it was a place to live. Choose to live in God's provision and protection, for true security is found ultimately in him alone.

Be still my soul: the Lord is on thy side;
Bear patiently the cross of grief or pain;
Leave to thy God to order and provide;
In every change he faithful will remain.
Be still, my soul: thy best, thy heavenly friend
Through thorny ways leads to a joyful end.

Katharina Van Schlegel
(From Psalm 46:10)

A Moment to Refresh

Rock of ages, cleft for me, let me hide myself in Thee.

Augustus M. Toplady

What is the rock within which the heart of man can safely live? Has it been named? Has it not been called the Rock of Ages? And have not they who have fled to it been assured day by day of ever-increasing security? That rock is open to us all. Blessed are they who flee to it that they may find rest and sustenance.

Joseph Parker

It is the LORD who goes before you. He will be with you; he will not fail you or forsake you. Do not fear or be dismayed.

Deuteronomy 31:8 NRSV

God is our refuge and strength, A very present help in trouble. Therefore we will not fear, though the earth should change.

Psalm 46:1–2 NASB

We who have this spiritual treasure are like common clay pots, in order to show that the supreme power belongs to God, not to us. We are often troubled, but not crushed; sometimes in doubt, but never in despair; there are many enemies, but we are never without a friend; and though badly hurt at times, we are not destroyed.

2 Corinthians 4:7–9 GNT

The salvation of the righteous comes from the LORD; he is their stronghold in time of trouble. The LORD helps them and delivers them; he delivers them from the wicked and saves them, because they take refuge in him.

Psalm 37:39–40 NIV

TIME TO PLAY

A Moment to Rest

Children are masters of play. They take life as they find it and allow their imaginations to fill in the blanks. What other explanation can there be for their ability to sit happily in the dirt for hours with nothing more than a stick? How else could they transform a box into a cave or a car or a cruise ship? How else could they take a blanket and "see" a tent, a superhero cape, a landscape for a village?

One laugh of a child will make the holiest day more sacred.

Robert Green Ingersoll

Take a break from your busy schedule and watch your children play, or better yet—join them. Get down on the floor, go out into the yard, hop onto the merry-go-round at the park, or throw a few snowballs. Enter your child's world of imagination and rediscover the joy of make-believe. Revel in your child's delight—and your own—when you take the time to play.

Let your body and mind relax as you enter the carefree world of childhood. For a few short minutes, shake off the responsibilities and refinements of adulthood and allow yourself to be a kid. Reflect with delight on the fact that you are indeed a child—a child of God.

A Moment to Reflect

*[Jesus] took the children in his arms,
put his hands on them and blessed them.*

Mark 10:16 NIV

Children are capable of unfettered play because they are comfortable with their dependence on others. They know that someone will be watching out for them, and they accept that fact without question.

If the responsibilities of your grown-up world keep you running in circles, spinning plates, and trying to hold all the aspects of your life together, visualize yourself as a child at play under God's watchful eye. Forget your tension. Let worries drain away. Deliberately relax your shoulders, relax your stance, let your limbs hang loose. Know that God, who is more dependable than any earthly parent could ever be, is always looking out for you. So play! Enjoy God's world.

*Our religion is one which challenges the ordinary human
standards by holding that the ideal of life is the spirit of a
little child. We tend to glorify adulthood and wisdom and
worldly prudence, but the gospel reverses all this. The gospel
says that the inescapable condition of entrance into the divine
fellowship is that we turn and become as a little child.*

Elton Trueblood

*Just as parents are kind to their children,
the LORD is kind to all who worship him.*

Psalm 103:13 CEV

A Moment to Refresh

*Some people brought children to Jesus for him
to place his hands on them, but the disciples
scolded the people. When Jesus noticed this,
he was angry and said to his disciples,
"Let the children come to me, and do
not stop them, because the Kingdom
of God belongs to such as these."*

Mark 10:13–14 GNT

*[Jesus] called a little child and had him stand
among them. And he said: "I tell you the truth,
unless you change and become like little
children, you will never enter the
kingdom of heaven."*

Matthew 18:2–3 NIV

*How precious is Your lovingkindness, O God!
And the children of men take refuge
in the shadow of Your wings.
They drink their fill of the abundance
of Your house;
And You give them to drink of the
river of Your delights.
For with You is the fountain of life;
In Your light we see light.
O continue Your lovingkindness
to those who know You,
And Your righteousness to the
upright in heart.*

Psalm 36:7–10 NASB

*A world without
children is a world
without newness,
regeneration, color,
and vigor.*

James C. Dobson

*The soul is healed
by being with
children.*

Fyodor
Dostoyevsky

STARRY NIGHTS

A Moment to Rest

You might be surprised to discover the power of a starry night. Viewing the heavens that God has created is an inspiring event. And it's open to all. Simply step outside on a clear night, bring the kids along, throw a blanket on the ground, and get comfortable. Lie there in the darkness, take in the broad expanse of the sky, and watch together as dancing dots of brilliant light shimmer above, beneath, and around the silver orb of the moon. In comparison to such a startling display, family and personal problems often appear small and inconsequential, and possibilities great and unlimited.

On colder nights, wrap yourselves in blankets and sit on lawn chairs with coffee or hot chocolate. Scan the heavens from your earthbound vantage point as wonder and awe fill your hearts. Sense the vastness and intricacy of God's creation. Marvel at the power that holds all things together.

When I look at the night sky and see the work of your fingers — the moon and the stars you set in place — what are mere mortals that you should think about them, human beings that you should care for them? Yet you . . . crowned them with glory and honor.

Psalm 8:3–5 NLT

In moments like these your heart is most receptive to God's still, small voice—the voice that comes from within and envelops you with a sense of joy and thankfulness, the voice that tells you that you are more important to him than the moon and all the stars. You are the crowning achievement of all God's creation.

> *The LORD merely spoke, and the heavens were created.*
> *He breathed the word, and all the stars were born.*

Psalm 33:6 NLT

God created the heavens simply by speaking a word. And he created you—knit you together—in your mother's womb. No one can even begin to imagine the complexities of the universe or the intricacies of the human body. And yet the God who caused all things to be, who holds all things together by his power . . . loves you. You are his child. Consider the intensity of your love for your own child, and know that God's love is so much more. He wants to speak words deep inside your soul that can set you free from burdens and cares. But you've got to be still long enough to sense what he's saying.

You know that he cares—after all, he's written it in the sky. Take a moment to be quiet and let the wonder of his love sink in.

> *To say that God is Creator is another way of saying that he is Father; had he not been Father, he would not have been Creator. It was being Father that made him want to create. Because he was infinitely pleased in his Son, he wanted sons, and it was in the image of his Son that he made the world. His creation was an overflowing of love and delight.*

Louis Evely

> *The heavens are telling of the glory of God;*
> *And their expanse is declaring the work of His hands.*

Psalm 19:1 NASB

A Moment to Refresh

*Two things fill
me with constantly
increasing
admiration and
awe, the longer
and more
earnestly I reflect
on them; the
starry heavens
without and the
moral law within.*

Immanuel Kant

*When considering
the creation, the
how and the when
does not matter so
much as the why
and the wherefore.*

R. de Campoamor

*This is what the LORD says—your Redeemer,
who formed you in the womb: I am the LORD,
who has made all things, who alone
stretched out the heavens, who spread
out the earth by myself.*

Isaiah 44:24 NIV

*Our LORD, let the heavens now praise your
miracles, and let all of your angels
praise your faithfulness.*

Psalm 89:5 CEV

*Ever since God created the world, his invisible
qualities, both his eternal power and his divine
nature, have been clearly seen; they are
perceived in the things that God has made.*

Romans 1:20 GNT

*The LORD is God, and he created the heavens
and earth and put everything in place. He made
the world to be lived in, not to be a place of
empty chaos. "I am the LORD," he says, "and
there is no other. I publicly proclaim bold
promises. . . . I would not have told the people . . .
to seek me if I could not be found. I, the
LORD, speak only what is true and
declare only what is right."*

Isaiah 45:18–19 NLT

PEN AND INK

A Moment to Rest

When you write things down, it's usually so you won't forget them. Moms have tight schedules and lots of lists. How else are you going to keep up with dance class, football practice, choir practice, music lessons, library due dates, science fair projects, and groceries? But there are other important reasons—besides lists—for writing things down. One is that doing so releases your unique creativity and reenergizes your inner self.

> *In a very real sense, the writer writes in order to teach himself.*
>
> Alfred Kazin

Keeping a journal has long been a cherished activity. Many people, young and old, rich and poor, famous and obscure, have understood the power of writing their thoughts as a way of expressing themselves. You can journal in a spiral notebook, a leather-bound book, or on your PDA. And you can take as much or as little time as your schedule allows. Forget about style and grammar, spelling and punctuation. Just write as your heart speaks to you, delving down deep into your inner self.

Writing can help you discover so many things about yourself. It can help you identify your gifts and talents, those things that bring joy and fulfillment to your life. It can help you gain perspective and discover aspects of your temperament and personality that you never knew existed. Open your heart and mind and let your pen lead the way.

A Moment to Reflect

[The apostle John wrote:] "I write these things to you who believe in the name of the Son of God so that you may know that you have eternal life."

1 John 5:13 NIV

Writing your thoughts is a valuable tool for unburdening your mind and heart, sorting out solutions, and creating a record of personal and spiritual growth. And writing your thoughts makes you feel good. It also helps you to look back and see where you've been and how God has worked in your life so you can hope and pray about tomorrow.

If you have never enjoyed the sensation of a pen in your hand, to feel it slide smoothly across the paper, it could be time for you to discover this pleasant and therapeutic art. Select an appealing paper, a good pen, a naturally lighted corner, and a cozy chair. Now, for a few quiet moments, let the thoughts and words flow.

Let me trace my hope in symbols, let me move mountains within a phrase. Emotion's turbulent core, so threateningly close within, now becomes benign under the taming of my pen. Let me compose the letters of my heart. Let me ascribe them to beauty and delight. The lament of sorrow, so threateningly close within, now becomes benign under the taming of my pen.

Tara Afriat

The LORD said to Moses, "Write down these words, for in accordance with these words I have made a covenant with you and with Israel."

Exodus 34:27 NIV

*The One who was sitting on the throne said,
"Look! I am making everything new!" Then
he said, "Write this, because these
words are true and can be trusted."*

Revelation 21:5 NCV

*The LORD answered me and said,
"Record the vision
And inscribe it on tablets,
That the one who reads it may run.
For the vision is yet for the appointed time;
It hastens toward the goal and it will not fail.
Though it tarries, wait for it;
For it will certainly come, it will not delay."*

Habakkuk 2:2–3 NASB

*[The apostle Luke wrote:] "It seemed good to
me also, having had perfect understanding of
all things from the very first, to write to you an
orderly account . . . that you may know the
certainty of those things in which
you were instructed."*

Luke 1:3–4 NKJV

*My dear friends, be glad that you belong to the
Lord. It doesn't bother me to write the same
things to you that I have written before. In
fact, it is for your own good.*

Philippians 3:1 CEV

*Words, those
precious cups
of meaning.*

Augustine of Hippo

*There is no
lighter burden,
nor more
agreeable,
than a pen.*

Petrarch

THE ONE WORD YOU
NEED TO HEAR

A Moment to Rest

Crickets chirping beneath a star-filled sky, waves rushing toward a sandy shore, birds singing in a sparkling fountain—some sounds in nature have an amazing capacity to soothe our minds and reenergize our hearts. Imagine a few of your favorites as you spend a few quiet moments today. Then consider: Is there a word that could have the same effect on your inner being?

There is now no condemnation for those who are in Christ Jesus.

Romans 8:1 NASB

Much like the sounds of nature, the right phrases spoken just when we most need to hear them have an amazing capacity to soothe and restore. "I love you," "I'll be there," and "I'll help" are just a few. Yet one word you might not think of until you really need to hear it is the word *forgiven*. This one rarely used word holds the power of restoration like no other word on earth, for it can restore not only a heart or mind but a relationship as well.

Consider the last time your child disobeyed your instruction or behaved toward you in an unloving way. Do you remember how much your child needed to receive your forgiveness? You could probably see the relief on her face and feel the release in her body as you accepted her back into your arms, forgiven and restored.

A Moment to Reflect

"I, even I, am he who blots out your transgressions,
for my own sake, and remembers your
sins no more," [says the Lord.]

Isaiah 43:25 NIV

As a mom, you struggle with a dizzying array of demands each day. Try as you may, you simply cannot do it all and be it all perfectly, all of the time. As a result, you often feel the weight of others' criticism or even your own self-condemnation.

Did you know that today God offers a relationship in which you are not condemned? Whether you have failed in some area or whether you are simply feeling the weight of others' expectations, turn to God in prayer. Experience relief and release as he accepts you into his arms, forgiven and restored.

When condemnation speaks to me, and I feel bound,
When those I love most seem to feel I've let them down,
When my soul aches
And my heart breaks
With heaviness and fear,
I run to You for my rescue,
and Your arms draw me near.
Then You say, "Forgiven.
Child of Mine, find rest here. You are forgiven."

Melinda Mahand

If we confess our sins to God, he will keep his promise
and do what is right: he will forgive us our sins
and purify us from all our wrongdoing.

1 John 1:9 GNT

A Moment to Refresh

GOD is sheer mercy and grace. . . . So strong is his love to those who fear him. . . . As far as sunrise is from sunset, he has separated us from our sins. As parents feel for their children, GOD feels for those who fear him.

Psalm 103:8, 11–13
THE MESSAGE

In these days of guilt complexes, perhaps the most glorious word in the English language is forgiven.

Billy Graham

This is how much God loved the world: He gave his Son, his one and only Son. And this is why: so that no one need be destroyed; by believing in him, anyone can have a whole and lasting life. God didn't go to all the trouble of sending his Son merely to point an accusing finger, telling the world how bad it was. He came to help, to put the world right again.

John 3:16–17 THE MESSAGE

You are forgiving and good, O Lord, abounding in love to all who call to you. Hear my prayer, O LORD; listen to my cry for mercy. In the day of my trouble I will call to you, for you will answer me.

Psalm 86:5–7 NIV

By the blood of Christ we are set free, that is, our sins are forgiven. How great is the grace of God, which he gave to us in such large measure!

Ephesians 1:7–8 GNT

Blessed is the one whose transgression is forgiven, whose sin is covered. Blessed is the man against whom the LORD counts no iniquity, and in whose spirit there is no deceit.

Psalm 32:1–2 ESV

LONGING FOR ACCEPTANCE

A Moment to Rest

Take some time to go to a place of quietness, a place where you can be still and become aware of God's presence with you. Welcome God into these moments and sense his love for you.

Although you may need to pause often in order to sense God's presence, you have no need to pause to sense the presence of other people. You perceive their presence instantly.

Your awareness of their presence has a stronger impact than you may realize, for that presence speaks to one of your deepest human needs—the need to be accepted.

> *Christianity is about acceptance, and if God accepts me as I am, then I had better do the same for others.*
>
> Hugh Montefiore

You spend much of your time trying to receive acceptance from those in your presence. That desire influences everything from the way you speak to the way you dress. Even moms are prone to fine-tune an image so that it will be received with acceptance. As an adult, you simply have become so polished at it that you are less obvious doing it than are your older children.

Once again, God offers to meet you at the place of your deepest need. As his children, you are truly accepted, not for how you look or how you behave, but simply for who you are.

A Moment to Reflect

The LORD takes pleasure in those who fear Him,
In those who hope in His mercy.

Psalm 147:11 NKJV

Knowledge of God's acceptance can have a powerful impact on your prayer life. If you have struggled with feelings of inadequacy or inferiority that have kept you from God, understanding his acceptance frees you to go to him with confidence and thanksgiving today.

Yet God's acceptance has an impact not only on your life but also on the lives of those around you. Since God accepts you, he desires that you accept others. Acceptance is an appealing quality to a person who has never experienced it. Acceptance opened many doors for Jesus to teach people about God. It will open many doors for you to teach about him as well.

Whether men be pleased or displeased, whether they judge
you, or whatever they call you, it will seem a small matter
to you in comparison to God's judgment. You live not
on them. You can bear their displeasure,
censures, and reproaches, if God be but pleased.

Richard Baxter

Accept each other just as Christ has accepted you
so that God will be given glory.

Romans 15:7 NLT

Peter fairly exploded with his good news: "It's God's own truth, nothing could be plainer: God plays no favorites! It makes no difference who you are or where you're from—if you want God and are ready to do as he says, the door is open. The Message he sent to the children of Israel— that through Jesus Christ everything is being put together again—well, he's doing it everywhere, among everyone."

Acts 10:34–36 THE MESSAGE

Real love isn't our love for God, but his love for us. God sent his Son to be the sacrifice by which our sins are forgiven. Dear friends, since God loved us this much, we must love each other.

1 John 4:10–11 CEV

The LORD delights in his people; he crowns the humble with victory. Let the faithful rejoice that he honors them. Let them sing for joy as they lie on their beds. Let the praises of God be in their mouths.

Psalm 149:4–6 NLT

Let the words of my mouth, and the meditation of my heart, be acceptable in thy sight, O LORD, my strength, and my redeemer.

Psalm 19:14 KJV

We can do nothing if we hate ourselves, or feel that all our actions are doomed to failure because of our own worthlessness. We have to take ourselves, good and bad alike, on trust before we can do anything.

Martin Israel

Accept the fact that you are accepted.

Paul Tillich

A SONG FROM THE HEART

A Moment to Rest

Singing has been called the universal cure—all for what ails the soul. The beautiful part is that it doesn't matter how well or how badly a person sings; the remedy works either way.

You may not have the kind of voice that brings fame and fortune, but don't let that stop you. Break out into song, and do it often. If there's a song running around in your head, let it out. Even when you can't physically take a break, give yourself a refreshing interlude by singing a happy song anytime or anyplace you feel comfortable doing so—while driving, while working, while holding your child. Sing to your kids, with your kids, to your husband. If you don't know the words,

Let us go singing as far as we go; the road will be less tedious.

Virgil A. Kraft

that's not a problem either. Sing along with the radio, make up your own words to a familiar melody, or just hum.

As you sing, let your mind relax. Let the tension and stress in your body flow up and out. Allow the music to fill your being. Then when you've sung your silly songs and your happy songs, your folk songs and your love songs, sing a song of praise to God for giving you a song to sing and a voice to sing it with.

A Moment to Reflect

*O come, let us sing unto the LORD: let us make a joyful
noise to the rock of our salvation. Let us come before his
presence with thanksgiving, and make a joyful noise
unto him with psalms. For the LORD is a great God,
and a great King above all gods.*

Psalm 95:1–3 KJV

How many times have you watched your child at play and
heard snatches of song coming from her happy heart? Let
her teach you to sing about . . . everything.

Life is full of reasons to sing; God's delightful gift of song
was designed for you to enjoy. Throughout the ages men and
women have chosen music to communicate the longings,
celebrations, and sufferings inherent in being human. So go
ahead; express yourself with song. Let music fill your days.
Remember that Miriam sang and danced before the Lord.
David did the same. They allowed their inner rejoicing to
burst forth—the natural result was song. Rejoice in the good
times and the not-so-bad times, and loosen the occasional
tight grip of fear or anxiety with a song. Open your mouth,
fill your lungs with air, and burst forth with confidence, joy,
and thanksgiving.

*I sing the goodness of the Lord,
who filled the earth with food,
Who formed the creatures through the Word,
and then pronounced them good.
Lord, how Thy wonders are displayed,
wherever I turn my eye,
If I survey the ground I tread,
or gaze upon the sky.*

Isaac Watts

A Moment to Refresh

*A careless song,
with a little
nonsense in it
now and then, does
not misbecome
a monarch.*

Horace Walpole

*When your heart
is full of Christ,
you want to sing.*

Charles Haddon
Spurgeon

*Sing a new song to the LORD!
He has worked miracles,
and with his own powerful arm,
he has won the victory.*

Psalm 98:1 CEV

*[God] put a new song in my mouth, a song of
praise to our God. Many will see and fear,
and put their trust in the LORD.*

Psalm 40:3 NRSV

*Miriam . . . took a tambourine in her hand,
and all the women followed her, with tam-
bourines and dancing. Miriam sang to them:
"Sing to the LORD, for he is highly exalted."*

Exodus 15:20–21 NIV

*Shout praises to the LORD,
everyone on this earth.
Be joyful and sing as you come in
to worship the LORD!
You know the LORD is God!
He created us, and we belong to him;
we are his people, the sheep in his pasture.*

Psalm 100:1–3 CEV

TIME FOR TEA

A Moment to Rest

For centuries, tea has been the drink of choice for princes and paupers, wise men and fools, aristocrats and commoners. All have treasured it for its calming, relaxing qualities.

Brewing a cup of tea isn't necessarily quick or convenient, but it's worth the small inconvenience. It's definitely a drink to be savored, not gulped. So take a little time out of your action-packed day and enjoy a quiet moment or two with a cup of tea and a thankful heart.

Take a lesson from tea: Its real strength comes out when it gets into hot water.

Author Unknown

You can share this teatime with your kids; boys and girls alike will enjoy spending time with you. Pull out the tea set or some special mugs. Together, you can relax and sip and say what's on your minds. Or you can enjoy that cup of tea with a friend as the kids play or go about their usual routine. And don't forget to let your mind dwell on all that God has done for you.

So put on the teapot and relax. Find a soothing spot to enjoy your cup of hot, freshly brewed tea. Sip it slowly, allowing the soothing taste and aroma to comfort you. Let your mind drift freely as you rest and reenergize yourself.

A Moment to Reflect

> *Whatever you do, whether you eat*
> *or drink, do it all for God's glory.*

1 Corinthians 10:31 GNT

God is aware of the complexities and stress-filled circumstances that you face in your life. He cares when your son outgrows his shoes overnight, when you have a flat tire on the way to work, or when you worry about the argument you had with a friend.

God cares so much that he has provided many ways for you to reenergize with natural foods that can strengthen and renew your body and mind and help you relax. Tea is just one of them.

When you find yourself feeling the stress, boil the water, steep the tea, and sit for a quiet moment, allowing yourself to enjoy the simple pleasure of a cup of tea. Use this time to tell God about the stressors you face and to thank him for the good things he has provided.

> *Yellow leaves dance upon the chilly ground*
> *Autumn gusts its last goodbye*
> *To summer sunshine, green, and warmth*
> *While I, cozy inside, put on the kettle and*
> *Ready the table with sweets that delight*
> *And the cup that awaits my ritual of tea.*

Tara Afriat

> *Oh, taste and see that the LORD is good!*
> *Blessed is the man who takes refuge in him!*

Psalm 34:8 ESV

I will bless the LORD at all times;
his praise shall continually be in my mouth.
My soul makes its boast in the LORD;
let the humble hear and be glad.
Oh, magnify the LORD with me, and let us
exalt his name together!

Psalm 34:1–3 ESV

God said, "Behold, I have given you every plant
yielding seed that is on the surface of all the
earth, and every tree which has fruit yielding
seed; it shall be food for you."

Genesis 1:29 NASB

Your righteousness is like
the mountains of God;
Your judgments are like a great deep.
O LORD, You preserve man and beast.
How precious is Your lovingkindness, O God!
And the children of men take refuge
in the shadow of Your wings.
They drink their fill of the
abundance of Your house;
And You give them to drink of the
river of Your delights.

Psalm 36:6–8 NASB

Thank God for
tea! What did the
world do without
tea? How did it
exist? I am glad
I was not born
before tea.

Sydney Smith

He who has health
has hope, and he
who has hope
has everything.

Ancient Proverb

UNAFRAID

A Moment to Rest

On this day, wait until evening to find some time to be alone for a while. Go outdoors and take in the peaceful elements that come with the dusk—the chorus of night-time animals, the cool evening breeze, perhaps even a gentle twilight shower.

> *We must welcome the night. It's the only time that the stars shine.*
>
> Michel Quoist

This setting that signals such peace and tranquillity sometimes brings with it a multitude of worries and fears. Just as children sometimes do, moms also may lie anxious in bed. In the darkness of nighttime, your heart and mind seem especially susceptible to troubling voices that recount the unfinished tasks of the day, the litany of demands that tomorrow brings, the potential struggles or trials in your future, and the never-ending supply of what-ifs.

Yet unlike your children, you do not feel the freedom to cry out in the night, to run to the side of someone who loves you and exclaim, "I'm afraid." Instead you toss and turn and add yet one more sleepless night to the tally.

In these restless moments, you often feel alone and vulnerable. But you don't have to. God longs for you to run to him for comfort, protection, hope, relief from fear. Imagine yourself as God's child, running to him for safety, for the reassurance that he is there and all will be well. His love and protection are all around you. In his presence, there is no reason for fear.

*God's peace, which is so great we cannot understand it,
will keep your hearts and minds in Christ Jesus.*

Philippians 4:7 NCV

Darkness or light, nighttime or day—such variations do not alter God's presence. Yet they often alter your human thoughts and emotions. Whether in a time of literal darkness or of spiritual darkness, meditate on the verses on the following pages. Spend your time praying and meditating. Keep a Bible beside your bed, for nothing has the power to dispel fear and uncertainty like God's Word.

God is present, even in the darkness, and he will respond when we turn to him for comfort and help.

If you happen to fall asleep as you spend time with God, there is no need to feel guilt. You have just found how to rest in his arms.

*Be thou my vision, O Lord of my heart; naught be all else to
me, save that thou art—thou my best thought, by day or by
night, waking or sleeping, thy presence my light.*

Irish Poem, Circa 700
Versified by Mary Elizabeth Byrne,
Translated by Eleanor H. Hull

*I will lie down and sleep in peace, for you alone,
O LORD, make me dwell in safety.*

Psalm 4:8 NIV

A Moment to Refresh

I would rather walk with God in the dark than go alone in the light.

Mary Gardiner
Brainard

Faith grows only in the dark. You've got to trust him when you can't trace him. That's faith.

Lyell Rader

The Word was the source of life, and this life brought light to people. The light shines in the darkness, and the darkness has never put it out. . . . The Word became a human being and, full of grace and truth, lived among us. We saw his glory, the glory which he received as the Father's only Son.

John 1:4–5, 14 GNT

This is the message we have heard from Him and announce to you, that God is Light, and in Him there is no darkness at all. If we say that we have fellowship with Him and yet walk in the darkness, we lie and do not practice the truth; but if we walk in the Light as He Himself is in the Light, we have fellowship with one another, and the blood of Jesus His Son cleanses us from all sin.

1 John 1:5–7 NASB

Who among you fears the LORD and obeys the word of his servant? Let him who walks in the dark, who has no light, trust in the name of the LORD and rely on his God.

Isaiah 50:10 NIV

ALWAYS CLOSE BY

A Moment to Rest

Enjoy a change of pace as you pause to spend a few moments in quiet stillness. Even as you slip away for this precious time alone, recognize that God is always close by. Invite him to share these moments of rest and meditation.

Discovering time to be alone seems especially difficult for busy moms. The daily tasks of maintaining a home and raising a family compel you to spend far more time caring for the needs of others than you spend caring for your own. Often one of the first areas to suffer is time spent with God. How can you find time for prayer when brushing your teeth without interruption is a rare treat?

God is always near you and with you; leave Him not alone.

Brother
Lawrence

Fortunately, God does not demand that you be alone or that you be otherwise unoccupied in order to talk with him. He is always present with you, ready to listen and to respond to you. Your challenge is to become consciously aware of his presence on a daily, moment-by-moment basis. He is with you as you drive the car, take a shower, or prepare dinner for your family. So rather than waiting until you are alone and unoccupied to speak to him, you can begin a conversation anytime and anywhere you choose.

A Moment to Reflect

> *Let us . . . approach the throne of grace with*
> *confidence, so that we may receive mercy and*
> *find grace to help us in our time of need.*

Hebrews 4:16 NIV

Imagine calling a good friend on the phone and never hanging up. That kind of communication is possible with God. He actually is a friend, always intimately near you, and he invites you to keep the lines of communication open during your daily activities. This type of constant communication with God is exactly what the apostle Paul had in mind when he said to "pray continually" (1 Thessalonians 5:17 NIV).

You want your child to tell you where it hurts, how he feels, what's new in his world. God wants that kind of interaction with you. Let conversation with him become comfortable and regular; you will receive instruction, protection, communion, provision—whatever the needs of your heart—as you learn to recognize he is ever near.

> *When we sing, "Draw me nearer, nearer, blessed Lord," we*
> *are not thinking of the nearness of place, but of the nearness*
> *of relationship. It is for increasing degrees of awareness that*
> *we pray for a more perfect consciousness of the divine*
> *Presence. We need never shout across the spaces to*
> *an absent God. He is nearer than our own soul,*
> *closer than our most secret thoughts.*

A. W. Tozer

> *Now in Christ Jesus you who once were far off have*
> *been brought near by the blood of Christ.*

Ephesians 2:13 NKJV

*Let us draw near with a sincere heart in full
assurance of faith, having our hearts sprinkled
clean from an evil conscience and our bodies
washed with pure water. Let us hold fast the
confession of our hope without wavering,
for He who promised is faithful.*

Hebrews 10:22–23 NASB

*The LORD is righteous in all His ways,
Gracious in all His works.
The LORD is near to all who call upon Him,
To all who call upon Him in truth.
He will fulfill the desire of those who fear Him;
He also will hear their cry and save them.*

Psalm 145:17–19 NKJV

*Long ago the LORD said to Israel:
"I have loved you, my people,
with an everlasting love.
With unfailing love I have
drawn you to myself."*

Jeremiah 31:3 NLT

*The LORD is near to those who are discouraged;
he saves those who have lost all hope. Good
people suffer many troubles, but the LORD
saves them from them all.*

Psalm 34:18–19 GNT

*What our Lord
did was done with
this intent, and
this alone, that he
might be with us
and we with him.*

Meister Eckhart

*God, who is
everywhere,
never leaves us.*

Thomas Merton

HOLDING HIS HAND

A Moment to Rest

Allow yourself to lean back and reminisce about times you have held the hand of someone you love. Recall the deep feelings of acceptance and security that those moments offered. Remember the welcome realization that you were not alone on life's journey.

> *The LORD directs the steps of the godly. He delights in every detail of their lives. Though they stumble, they will never fall, for the LORD holds them by the hand.*
>
> Psalm 37:23–24
> NLT

Although the gesture of taking someone's hand seems simple, it often can fulfill physical, emotional, and even spiritual needs. For when two people join hands, they join hearts as well.

One such moment took place when Lisa's son was two years old. A forested embankment behind their home led to a shallow, spring-fed creek. Although Lisa's son begged daily to splash his toes in the cool, crystal clear water, she dared not let him head down the bank alone. She knew his unsteady legs and the steep grade of the hill would result in his being hurled headlong down the bank and face-first into the water.

So each day Lisa simply took her son by the hand and walked with him down the hill. Although stumbling was still a distinct possibility, she knew her son would not fall because his hand was securely clasped in hers. Lisa knew her child would be safe because he was not alone.

A Moment to Reflect

*I am the LORD your God. I am holding your hand,
so don't be afraid. I am here to help you.*

Isaiah 41:13 CEV

Today God is offering to take your hand and walk beside you on life's journey. He wants to be not only your companion but your guide and protector as well. Although you may be hurt by an occasional stumble, you will not be destroyed by a head-long fall as long as you are walking hand in hand with him.

Choose to take God's hand and join your heart with his. Just as a toddling child becomes more and more sure of his steps as he holds a parent's hand, so your steps will become more confident as you trust God to keep you safe. He will meet all your needs, and you will experience the incredible reality that you are not alone.

*Hand in hand with one who loves me,
Hand in hand, I safely go
Through the valleys of life's journey,
Then on to new heights in my soul.
Hand in hand with one who loves me,
Hand in hand, I am secure
As my father ever gently
Guides my steps and makes them sure.*

Melinda Mahand

[Jesus said,] "I give [my followers] eternal life, and they shall never perish; no one can snatch them out of my hand. My Father, who has given them to me, is greater than all; no one can snatch them out of my Father's hand."

John 10:28–29 NIV

A Moment to Refresh

God, the LORD, created the
heavens and stretched them out.
He created the earth and everything in it.
He gives breath to everyone,
life to everyone who walks the earth.
And it is he who says,
"I, the LORD, have called you to
demonstrate my righteousness.
I will take you by the hand and guard you."

Isaiah 42:5–6 NLT

To [God] who is able to keep you from falling
and to present you before his glorious presence
without fault and with great joy—to the only
God our Savior be glory, majesty, power and
authority, through Jesus Christ our Lord,
before all ages, now and forevermore!

Jude 24–25 NIV

O LORD, you protect me and save me; your care
has made me great, and your power has
kept me safe. You have kept me from being
captured, and I have never fallen.

Psalm 18:35–36 GNT

If I rise on the wings of the dawn, if I settle on
the far side of the sea, even there your hand will
guide me, your right hand will hold me fast.

Psalm 139:9–10 NIV

*No one is safe by
his own strength,
but he is safe by
the grace and
mercy of God.*

Cyprian

*Great eagles fly
alone; great lions
hunt alone; great
souls walk
alone—alone
with God.*

Leonard Ravenhill

WORTH THE WAIT

A Moment to Rest

For a few minutes today, step away from your fast-paced world. Find a place to pause and rest for a while, waiting for God to speak to your heart.

All of nature teaches us to wait. The dormant seed patiently awaits the return of spring. The songbird watches for each new dawn. Your child remains in the safety of your body until it's time for her to be born. Even the lowly caterpillar bides her time within a lonely chrysalis chamber until new wings form and signal the moment of her emergence. Some things are worth waiting for.

> *I will watch for the LORD; I will wait confidently for God, who will save me. My God will hear me.*
>
> Micah 7:7 GNT

What events have been worth waiting for in your life? Finding a life partner? Welcoming your newborn? Hearing your son's first word? Celebrating your daughter's first day of school? Attending your best friend's wedding? Regardless of which events come to mind, the aspect that made each wait worthwhile was not the event itself, but the intimate relationship that was inherent in the event. The loved one, the friend, the child was worth waiting for.

Likewise, God asks us to wait for him, not because he wants to inconvenience us or frustrate us, but because he wants a relationship with us. As we wait on God, we learn to trust, to hope, to rejoice, to know him. Knowing him more fully is always worth the wait.

A Moment to Reflect

Faith is the assurance of things hoped for,
the conviction of things not seen.

Hebrews 11:1 ESV

Is God keeping you waiting today? Is there a need you expressed or a request you made that seems to have been met with silence? Use this time to wait quietly for him to speak to your heart. Ask him to reveal to your deepest self the person he wants you to be, to give you a vision of his plans for you.

When you read about women in the Bible—Sarah, Rachel, Hannah, Elizabeth, Anna—many of them waited all their lives for God to answer the desires of their hearts. They looked forward to God's promises. They trusted that he knew what he was doing and that he would do what he said he would. If you are experiencing a period of waiting, live each day with hope and expectancy, because God always responds to those who wait.

I charge my thoughts, be humble still,
All my carriage mild,
Content, my Father, with Thy will,
And quiet as a child.
The patient soul, the lowly mind
Shall have a large reward:
Let saints in sorrow lie resigned,
And trust a faithful Lord.

Isaac Watts

I waited patiently for the LORD;
And He inclined to me and heard my cry.
He brought me up out of the pit of
destruction, out of the miry clay,
And He set my feet upon a rock
making my footsteps firm.
He put a new song in my mouth,
a song of praise to our God;
Many will see and fear
And will trust in the LORD.

Psalm 40:1–3 NASB

I am confident I will see the LORD's goodness
while I am here in the land of the living.
Wait patiently for the LORD.
Be brave and courageous.
Yes, wait patiently for the LORD.

Psalm 27:13–14 NLT

We were saved, and we have this hope.
If we see what we are waiting for,
that is not really hope.
People do not hope for something
they already have. But we are
hoping for something we do not
have yet, and we are waiting
for it patiently.

Romans 8:24–25 NCV

There is no
place for faith if
we expect God to
fulfill immediately
what he promises.

John Calvin

We must wait for
God, long, meekly,
in the wind and
wet, in the thunder
and lightning, in
the cold and the
dark. Wait, and
he will come.
He never comes
to those who
do not wait.

Frederick William
Faber

A PLACE FOR HOPE

A Moment to Rest

For a few minutes today, plan to experience the simple pleasure of quietness. As you begin to relax, turn your thoughts
to the things in life that bring you hope. What are your hopes
for yourself today? What are your hopes for tomorrow?

Think about your own children—innocent and passionate
in their hopes for the future. They eagerly anticipate such
modest events as taking a turn in a game
or making a batch of cookies or going to
visit their grandparents. They regard these
simple delights with great expectation
and confidence. They wholeheartedly
hope with no thought of failure or disappointment.

Never deprive
someone of
hope—it may
be all they have.

Author Unknown

Why do you suppose they hope so effort-
lessly? Perhaps because your loving fam-
ily relationships taught them it was safe to trust. Trust is, in
fact, the foundation on which hope is built. A person who
has learned to trust is able to hope.

Somewhere between childhood and adulthood you may
have lost your innocence and passion regarding hope. You
may have experienced disappointments in your relationships. You may have learned that hope can be ill-founded
or misplaced, and you may have ceased to trust. You may
have even ceased to hope. But God is the source of all hope,
and he wants you to overflow with it—sure in the knowledge that he is trustworthy, though others may not be.

A Moment to Reflect

*I will hope continually and will praise you yet more and
more. My mouth will tell of your righteous acts,
of your deeds of salvation all the day, for their
number is past my knowledge.*

Psalm 71:14–15 ESV

Today God offers you a relationship with him. A relationship
in which you can place your absolute confidence. His joy is
to fill your heart with great expectation and to teach you
once again to innocently, passionately hope . . . in him and
what he is able to do.

No matter what you face—financial struggles, a child's learning disability, loss of your spouse, overwhelming responsibilities—you can trust God in everything and in every way.
You can choose to wholeheartedly throw yourself into relationship with him. Ask him to re-create in your heart a place
for hope. His love will not fail or disappoint you. He will be
your hope and will satisfy your deepest longings.

*In Thee, therefore, O Lord God, I put all my hope and my
refuge, on Thee I lay all my tribulation and anguish. . . .
For many friends shall not profit, nor strong helpers be able
to succor, nor prudent counselors to give a useful answer, nor
the books of the learned to console, nor any precious sub-
stance to deliver, nor any secret and beautiful place to give
shelter, if Thou Thyself do not assist, help, strengthen,
comfort, instruct, keep in safety.*

Thomas à Kempis

Why are you downcast, O my soul? Why so disturbed within me? Put your hope in God, for I will yet praise him, my Savior and my God.

Psalm 43:5 NIV

The future is as bright as the promises of God.

Adoniram Judson

Let us give thanks to the God and Father of our Lord Jesus Christ! Because of his great mercy he gave us new life by raising Jesus Christ from death. This fills us with a living hope, and so we look forward to possessing the rich blessings that God keeps for his people. He keeps them for you in heaven, where they cannot decay or spoil or fade away.

1 Peter 1:3–4 GNT

We must accept finite disappointment, but we must never lose infinite hope.

Martin Luther King Jr.

Such things were written in the Scriptures long ago to teach us. And the Scriptures give us hope and encouragement as we wait patiently for God's promises to be fulfilled.

Romans 15:4 NLT

"I say this because I know what I am planning for you," says the LORD. "I have good plans for you, not plans to hurt you. I will give you hope and a good future."

Jeremiah 29:11 NCV

DARE TO DREAM

The dreams you dream are a prelude to greatness. They challenge, inspire, and give purpose to your life. Taking time out to dream of what could be is the first step toward making dreams become reality. Your children aren't afraid to dream. They seem to enter life with a limitless ability to see themselves as superheroes, great teachers, champion athletes, moms with twelve children. If it's possible, your child knows how to dream it.

In the midst of your long, busy day, take a break and let your heart fly free. If you can, find a comfortable place to do your dreaming. Take a walk in the park during your lunch break, enjoy your porch swing on a sunny day, settle in with a cup of tea while your children are napping, or just turn off the television and soak in the silence for a few minutes.

Hope is a waking dream.
Augustine of Hippo

Once you're comfortable, turn your thoughts to what you enjoy most. If it's writing, imagine yourself as an author; if it's being a great mom, see yourself developing new ways to draw out the potential in each of your children. As your dreams take shape, don't just dash off to the next thing; stay for a while. The first step to making your dreams come true is to make them your own.

A Moment to Reflect

Hope deferred makes the heart sick,
but a dream fulfilled is a tree of life.

Proverbs 13:12 NLT

Dreaming keeps hope alive in your life. And hope is to the spirit what water is to the body. It refreshes and renews.

If you have felt the joy of living slipping through your fingers, a dream session might be just what you need. Get started right away, and give yourself time, because most dreams take a while to come fully into being. Remember to ask God to inspire your dreams. He is eager to fill your heart with the full intent of his marvelous plans for your life. Don't put limits on what God wants for your future.

As I was sitting all alone
A star in yonder window shone
And led me to a place quite lovely
Where all my dreams circled above me
Each one was close enough to touch
Each goal that I desired so much
And hope soared high within my soul
I can't say why. I just know that I know.
Doubts and fears assail me still
But I stay near that window sill
And focus on that brilliant star
For that is where my victories are.

Roberta S. Cully

We are God's workmanship, created in Christ Jesus to do
good works, which God prepared in advance for us to do.

Ephesians 2:10 NIV

God is working in you, giving you the desire and the power to do what pleases him.

Philippians 2:13 NLT

The LORD spoke to Abram in a vision, "Abram, don't be afraid! I will protect you and reward you greatly."

Genesis 15:1 CEV

The way of the righteous is like the first gleam of dawn, which shines ever brighter until the full light of day.

Proverbs 4:18 NLT

In a vision one night, Daniel was shown the dream and its meaning. Then he praised the God who rules from heaven: "Our God, your name will be praised forever and forever. You are all-powerful, and you know everything. You control human events—you give rulers their power and take it away, and you are the source of wisdom and knowledge. You explain deep mysteries, because even the dark is light to you."

Daniel 2:19–22 CEV

Dream the impossible dream. Dreaming it may make it possible. It often has.

Author Unknown

Vision encompasses vast vistas outside the realm of the predictable, the safe, the expected.

Charles Swindoll

SOAKING IT UP

A Moment to Rest

Though they typically take a bit longer than a shower, baths are a wonderful way to relax. Take advantage of an opportunity when everyone is out of the house or when someone else is around to keep an eye on the kids. Turn off the phone and hide from the world for a few minutes. Climb in and slip down into the warm, soothing water. Allow the water to cover you all the way to your chin like a warm comforter.

> *Bathe twice a day to be really clean, once a day to be passably clean, once a week to avoid being a public menace.*
>
> Anthony Burgess

Close your eyes and let your mind drift away from problems, cares, and concerns. As you feel your body relaxing, focus your mind on God. Ask him to cleanse you from every unhealthy thought or action and refresh and restore your spirit with thoughts of goodness, gentleness, joy, and peace. Think about all the good things he has given you, and let your heart and mind be full of thankfulness.

A brisk shower cleanses and comforts the body, but taking time for a warm bath provides an opportunity to cleanse and comfort your heart. Lingering in a warm bath won't be possible every day. But try to sneak away a couple of times a week or on the weekend. Enjoy the feeling of being clean and refreshed inside as well as out.

A Moment to Reflect

Let us purify ourselves from everything that makes
body or soul unclean, and let us be completely
holy by living in awe of God.

2 Corinthians 7:1 GNT

A good soaking is helpful for the body, but even more important is the cleansing of your inner self. Focus your mind on the purifying truths found in Scripture, and ask God to use those truths to wash away the things in your life that shouldn't be there.

God sent Jesus to live in our world so that we could understand truth. Jesus himself declared, "I am . . . the truth" (John 14:6 NKJV). Let God's truth cleanse you and renew your heart. No matter what you've done, or what's been done to you, or how you feel you've failed, God's promise to you is sparkling-clean newness. Thank God that his power makes you truly clean.

If only for these rare and fleeting moments
I remove from myself all that clings to me,
Harries my thoughts, and burdens my soul when I
Fall into the water's warm embrace; released
Like a child from her mother's womb,
I emerge from my private baptism
And life greets me anew.

Tara Afriat

Cleanse me with hyssop, and I will be clean;
[O Lord,] wash me, and I will be whiter than snow.

Psalm 51:7 NIV

A Moment to Refresh

Christ is the God over all, who has arranged to wash away sin from mankind, rendering the old man new.

Hippolytus

Water clear, standing near, Wash our hands and faces clean. May the Lord, by His Word, Wash our hearts from every sin. So let everything we see Turn our thoughts, O Lord, to Thee.

Philip P. Bliss

Let's come near God with pure hearts and a confidence that comes from having faith. Let's keep our hearts pure, our consciences free from evil, and our bodies washed with clean water.

Hebrews 10:22 CEV

Christ loved the church and gave himself up for her to make her holy, cleansing her by the washing with water through the word.

Ephesians 5:25–26 NIV

*Have mercy upon me, O God,
According to Your lovingkindness;
According to the multitude of
Your tender mercies,
Blot out my transgressions.
Wash me thoroughly from my iniquity,
And cleanse me from my sin. . . .
Create in me a clean heart, O God,
And renew a steadfast spirit within me.*

Psalm 51:1–2, 10 NKJV

If we confess our sins to him, he is faithful and just to forgive us and to cleanse us from every wrong.
1 John 1:9 NLT

HANDCRAFTED

A Moment to Rest

Take some time today to absorb the beauty of God's creation. Isn't it amazing that every leaf unfolding, every cloud passing by, every insect buzzing—every created thing—is custom-designed by God? Watch your son as he rides his bike or your daughter as she swings. Marvel at the way their bodies move and work. Think back to the first moment you saw your child—the amazingly tiny and delicate being you held in your arms. Scripture teaches that each person is custom-designed and handcrafted by God. Think of all that truth implies.

> *We are the handiwork of God.*
>
> A. W. Tozer

What do you enjoy creating? Do you paint, cook, landscape, or play an instrument? Do you prefer to make crafts with your kids? Do you decorate, sing, knit, or sew? Do you write, quilt, or refinish furniture? Whatever your creative outlet, consider the extent to which the work of your hands is a work of self-expression and of love. To that same extent and more, you are the work of God's hands and as such are an expression of him and of his love.

Recognize that you, as God's workmanship, have high value. Begin today to discover his purposes for you. By fulfilling his purposes, you have the potential to affect not only life on earth, but life in eternity as well.

A Moment to Reflect

Your hands made me and fashioned me;
Give me understanding, that I may learn
Your commandments.

Psalm 119:73 NASB

You may tend to look in the mirror and find flaws. You may look at the abilities and talents of others and feel that you were left out. If you've watched others lead, achieve, create, shine . . . you may wonder what you could possibly do that might have significance. With children in the home, you may always be caring for their needs rather than accomplishing what someone else might consider "great things." Recognize today that God planned, designed, and made you by his own hand.

God created you thoughtfully and purposefully; he fashioned you specifically with your combination of personality and skills to accomplish his plans. Consider how to honor and care for yourself, his creation. Consider also how to fulfill the purposes he has for you, his creation. Thank God that you exist.

The next time you look into the mirror and feel inadequate
or inferior. . . . The next time you face a God-given
opportunity to minister in people's lives and feel challenged or
scared. . . . The next time you long with all your heart to
bring joy to God yet feel like you couldn't possibly do so. . . .
Just envision a label sewn onto your heart that reads:
"Handmade With Love by God."

Melinda Mahand

We are God's workmanship, created in Christ Jesus to do
good works, which God prepared in advance for us to do.

Ephesians 2:10 NIV

You made all the delicate, inner parts of my body and knit me together in my mother's womb. Thank you for making me so wonderfully complex! Your workmanship is marvelous—how well I know it. You watched me as I was being formed in utter seclusion, as I was woven together in the dark of the womb. You saw me before I was born. Every day of my life was recorded in your book. Every moment was laid out before a single day had passed.

Psalm 139:13–16 NLT

What are human beings that you are mindful of them, mortals that you care for them? Yet you have made them a little lower than God, and crowned them with glory and honor. You have given them dominion over the works of your hands; you have put all things under their feet.

Psalm 8:4–6 NRSV

*You are worthy, O Lord,
To receive glory and honor and power;
For You created all things,
And by Your will they exist and were created.*

Revelation 4:11 NKJV

My body was made for the love of God. Every cell in my body is a hymn to my creator and a declaration of love.

Ernesto Cardenal

God does not love us because we are valuable. We are valuable because God loves us.

Fulton John Sheen

ANGELS AT YOUR SIDE

A Moment to Rest

Let the burdens and tensions of your day drift away. Look slowly to your left and to your right. Do you notice angels at your side? Probably not. Having angels there is not unusual—but actually being aware of them is.

Consider for a moment how the word *angel* is commonly used in day-to-day life. Helpful friends, sleeping children, and even loved ones in heaven may sometimes be called "angels." Angels have been portrayed as chubby, childlike beings with wings who flutter around doing good things.

> *Beside each believer stands an angel as protector and shepherd leading him to life.*
>
> Basil the Great

Yet the Bible teaches that angels are, in reality, none of these things. They are fierce and wonderful creatures. In the Bible, angels sometimes appeared as humans, and they struck fear in the men and women who saw them. Other angelic beings are described as fantastic creatures with multiple wings and faces and eyes. Angels were created by God to worship and serve him, to act as his messengers, and to carry out his purposes on earth. Angels, in fact, are especially active in the lives of God's people. They fed Elijah in the wilderness, ministered to Jesus after his temptation, delivered messages to God's children, and actively protected them. As you ponder the hosts around us, thank God for *all* his creation—including the angels in our midst.

A Moment to Reflect

The angel of the LORD is a guard; he surrounds and defends all who fear him. Taste and see that the LORD is good. Oh, the joys of those who take refuge in him!

Psalm 34:7–8 NLT

The next time you wonder whether you are really important to God, remember that of all the tasks his angels could perform, God sends them to take care of you. Just as the president of the United States has Secret Service agents and famous or wealthy people have their bodyguards, so God has placed angels by your side to guard and protect you.

This truth is a powerful statement of your importance in God's eyes! You are precious to him. You are valuable to him. You are loved by him. So loved that he has provided an army of powerful spirit beings—angels—to surround the children of God.

Everlasting God, you have ordained and constituted in a wonderful order the ministries of angels and mortals: Mercifully grant that as your holy angels always serve and worship you in heaven, so by your appointment they may help and defend us here on earth, through Jesus Christ our Lord, who lives and reigns with you and the Holy Spirit, one God, for ever and ever. Amen.

The Book of Common Prayer

[God] will command his angels concerning you to guard you in all your ways.

Psalm 91:11 NIV

A Moment to Refresh

Sweet souls around us watch us still, Press nearer to our side; Into our thoughts, into our prayers, With gentle helpings glide.

Harriet Beecher Stowe

The servants of Christ are protected by invisible, rather than visible, beings. But if these guard you, they do so because they have been summoned by your prayers.

Ambrose

Are not all angels spirits in the divine service, sent to serve for the sake of those who are to inherit salvation?

Hebrews 1:14 NRSV

At the first light of dawn, the king got up and hurried to the lions' den. When he came near the den, he called to Daniel in an anguished voice, "Daniel, servant of the living God, has your God, whom you serve continually, been able to rescue you from the lions?" Daniel answered, "O king, live forever! My God sent his angel, and he shut the mouths of the lions. They have not hurt me, because I was found innocent in his sight."

Daniel 6:19–22 NIV

Keep on loving each other as brothers and sisters. Don't forget to show hospitality to strangers, for some who have done this have entertained angels without realizing it!

Hebrews 13:1–2 NLT

[God said to the Israelites,] "I am sending an angel ahead of you, who will protect you as you travel. He will lead you to the place I have prepared."

Exodus 23:20 NCV

LEAN ON GOD

A Moment to Rest

Take an opportunity simply to rest. Curl up somewhere comfortable and cozy. Lean back and let the tension melt from your muscles. Can you imagine your body resting this way if you did not have the cushions to lean against, the sofa to hold the weight of your body? Can you imagine your inner being finding rest if there was no place to lean, no one to trust, no one to help with all the worries and cares in your heart?

Pull your child into your lap and feel her body relax against you, getting comfortable, trusting you to hold her, telling you all about what she's been doing. As she leans into you, imagine yourself leaning into God's arms—with the assurance of a child.

> *God is not a deceiver, that he should offer to support us, and then, when we lean upon Him, should slip away from us.*
>
> Augustine of Hippo

Loved ones may sometimes be able to help with your worries or cares. They may lend a hand or lend an ear and lighten your load. But even with support from loved ones in your life, some burdens remain yours alone. And God's.

This truth is clearly illustrated in a letter that Paul wrote. He told God's people to "help carry one another's burdens" (Galatians 6:2 GNT), and then he followed that advice with a gentle reminder that "each of you have to carry your own load" (Galatians 6:5 GNT). Some burdens remain on your shoulders regardless of the attentive people in your life, and those burdens are ones only God can bear. Lean into him and let him hold you—and your burdens.

A Moment to Reflect

*My message and my preaching were . . . in demonstration
of the Spirit and of the power, so that your faith would not
rest on the wisdom of men, but on the power of God.*

1 Corinthians 2:4–5 NASB

What worries and concerns are weighing heavily on you?
Read the following verses of Scripture and hear God's plea
that you give those burdens to him. Notice he does not offer
to "help" you with the burdens; he offers to completely bear
them for you. He asks you to let go of them and let him have
them.

When you place your weight—the burden of your body—on
the sofa, you know that it isn't going to collapse under you
and let you fall. Just as you trust that your furniture will hold
your weight, so also trust God; he is able to hold the weight
of your soul's burdens. Tell him about each one and make
the conscious choice to leave the matter in his hands. Lean
on him.

What a fellowship, what a joy divine,
Leaning on the everlasting arms;
What a blessedness, what a peace is mine,
Leaning on the everlasting arms.

Elisha A. Hoffman

Give your burdens to the LORD, and he will take care of you.
He will not permit the godly to slip and fall.

Psalm 55:22 NLT

*Cast all your anxiety on him because he cares
for you. . . . And the God of all grace, who
called you to his eternal glory in Christ, after
you have suffered a little while, will himself
restore you and make you strong,
firm and steadfast.*

1 Peter 5:7, 10 NIV

*Thus says the LORD,
"Stand by the ways and see and
ask for the ancient paths,
Where the good way is, and walk in it;
And you will find rest for your souls."*

Jeremiah 6:16 NASB

*[Jesus said,] "Come to Me, all you who labor
and are heavy laden, and I will give you rest.
Take My yoke upon you and learn from Me,
for I am gentle and lowly in heart, and
you will find rest for your souls."*

Matthew 11:28–29 NKJV

*Thus said the Lord GOD, the Holy One of
Israel: In returning and rest you shall
be saved; in quietness and in trust
shall be your strength.*

Isaiah 30:15 NRSV

*Every thing a man
leans upon but
God, will be a dart
that will certainly
pierce his heart
through and
through. He, who
leans only upon
Christ, lives the
highest, choicest,
safest, and
sweetest life.*

Thomas Brooks

*Jesus knows we
must come apart
and rest awhile, or
else we may just
plain come apart.*

Vance Havner

EXPRESS YOURSELF

A Moment to Rest

Perhaps you need a change of pace today, a time to slow down, gather your thoughts, and refresh your inner self. Take a break now to rest your body and quiet your mind for a few moments. Consider how amazing God's plan for your physical and mental being is. He created you in such a way that something as simple as rest can answer the needs of your body and spirit, bringing restoration and renewal.

You answer us with awesome deeds of righteousness, O God our Savior, the hope of all the ends of the earth and of the farthest seas.

Psalm 65:5 NIV

Yet not every need is answered quite so simply. Sometimes your needs can loom like a mountain before you. They require answers that seem impossible. They require might that is miraculous. They require nothing less than action from an all-powerful God.

As a mother, however, you have become used to being the one who answers questions and meets the needs and requests of your family. You are often the last person to express your needs or to ask for assistance. As a result, you are likely to be slow in turning to God for answers for yourself.

Today, be reminded that God is available to listen to *your* requests. So express yourself. He truly wants to hear your requests, and he promises to answer them, not with comforting platitudes but with awesome deeds.

A Moment to Reflect

*When I was in trouble, I called to the LORD,
and he answered me.*

Psalm 120:1 GNT

What are your needs at this moment? Do you face a situation
that seems insurmountable? Do you need an answer that is
awesome? If so, have you told God about it?

As a mom, one of your greatest desires is to meet your child's
needs. When he comes to you with a request, you long to
provide for him in the best way you can. Your God loves you
so much more than you love your own child. He wants to
provide for *you*, so express yourself. Tell God about the needs
in your life—large or small. Nothing that concerns your
heart is insignificant to him. Ask him to act on your behalf.
Give your cares to God; release your worries, your fears.
When you do, he has promised to deliver tangible help and
to work in wondrous ways. He is strong and able.

*I got up early one morning
And rushed right into the day;
I had so much to accomplish
That I didn't have time to pray.
Problems just tumbled about me,
And heavier came each task;
"Why doesn't God help me?" I wondered.
He answered, "You didn't ask."
I woke up early this morning,
And paused before entering the day;
I had so much to accomplish
That I had to take time to pray.*

Author Unknown

A Moment to Refresh

We should believe nothing is too small to be named before God. What should we think of the patient who told his doctor he was ill, but never went into particulars?

J. C. Ryle

God will always give what is right to his people who cry to him night and day, and he will not be slow to answer them. I tell you, God will help his people quickly.

Luke 18:7–8 NCV

You were in serious trouble, but you prayed to the LORD, and he rescued you. He brought you out of the deepest darkness and broke your chains. You should praise the LORD for his love and for the wonderful things he does for all of us.

Psalm 107:13–15 CEV

A prayer warrior is a person who is convinced that God is omnipotent — that God has the power to do anything, to change anyone, and to intervene in any circumstance. A person who truly believes this refuses to doubt God.

Author Unknown

Blessed is the man who always fears the LORD, but he who hardens his heart falls into trouble. . . . A faithful man will be richly blessed, but one eager to get rich will not go unpunished.

Proverbs 28:14, 20 NIV

Jesus answered saying to them, "Have faith in God. Truly I say to you, whoever says to this mountain, 'Be taken up and cast into the sea,' and does not doubt in his heart, but believes that what he says is going to happen, it will be granted him."

Mark 11:22–23 NASB

BREATHING—THE RHYTHM OF LIFE

A Moment to Rest

Inhale. Exhale. Inhale. Exhale. It's the rhythm of life, and yet it passes without effort, without thinking. When your baby is young, you watch for the rise and fall of his chest . . . trusting the rhythm to be there. When an aging pet lies still in a sunny spot, you wait to see her inhale, exhale. Each breath is a miracle, blessing our bodies and brains with the oxygen that brings life and sustenance. Perhaps that's why focused, deep breathing has such a calming, strengthening effect on both the body and the mind.

> *The LORD God formed the man from the dust of the ground and breathed into his nostrils the breath of life, and the man became a living being.*
>
> Genesis 2:7 NIV

The beauty of this exercise is that you don't need a special place or time to draw on its rich benefits. Just about any place is appropriate—in the middle of your busy day, as you wait to pick up your children, as you sit in a busy board meeting, even as you make a presentation. Simply take a deep breath, hold it for five seconds, and breathe out slowly through your nose. Do this once or several times in a row. As your lungs fill, oxygen rushes into your bloodstream and is carried to your brain and extremities. No one even needs to know that you are taking an oxygen break.

The results are instantaneous. You will quickly feel your nerves relaxing, your mood lifting, your fatigue abating—just by consciously doing what comes naturally.

A Moment to Reflect

Praise the LORD. Praise God in his sanctuary; praise him in his mighty heavens. Praise him for his acts of power; praise him for his surpassing greatness. . . . Let everything that has breath praise the LORD. Praise the LORD.

Psalm 150:1–2, 6 NIV

Each breath you take is a gift of life from God himself—an expression of his love for you and a reminder of his moment-by-moment commitment to you. How marvelous that he would invest so much in a simple, natural act.

If you have ever wondered if God cares about you, whether he is interested in the smallest details of your life, now you know. If you have ever wondered if he really wants to be part of your life every moment of every day, the answer is as close as your next breath.

God loves you. Breathe deeply and ponder that wonderful fact.

*One breath for every moment
The proof of life's bright flame,
Flowing always in and out,
Every day the same.
One breath for every moment
Sustaining life so sweet.
Giving strength to words and thoughts
While keeping up the beat.
One breath for every moment
A gift of God so true
Making each a living soul
As only God can do.*

Tara Afriat

A Moment to Refresh

*I will give thanks to You,
for I am fearfully and wonderfully made;
Wonderful are Your works,
And my soul knows it very well.*

Psalm 139:14 NASB

This is what God the LORD says — he who created the heavens and stretched them out, who spread out the earth and all that comes out of it, who gives breath to its people, and life to those who walk on it: "I, the LORD, have called you in righteousness; I will take hold of your hand. I will keep you and will make you to be a covenant for the people and a light for the Gentiles."

Isaiah 42:5–6 NIV

*How precious also are Your
thoughts to me, O God!
How great is the sum of them!
If I should count them, they would be
more in number than the sand;
When I awake, I am still with You.*

Psalm 139:17–18 NKJV

*[Jesus] said, "Peace be with you. As the
Father has sent me, so I am sending you."
Then he breathed on them and said,
"Receive the Holy Spirit."*

John 20:21–22 NLT

*The hand of God
is strong enough
to protect His
feeblest child, yet
gentle enough to
lead that same
child homeward.*

Melinda Mahand

*The life force is
vigorous. The
delight that
accompanies it
counter-balances
all the pains and
hardships that
confront men.
It makes life
worth living.*

W. Somerset
Maugham

UNFAILING POWER

A Moment to Rest

Modern moms have to move at a steady pace to get through each day. You need energy—a power source—to keep going until bedtime. Think about the energy the sun provides to the earth—energy for plants to make food, vitamin D for our bodies, light and warmth for all living creatures. Yes, the sun is one of God's many blessings to his creation, but it is also a spectacular illustration of his power.

You will never need more than God can supply.

J. I. Packer

Consider that the sun is large enough to contain more than one million Earths. At its center, the sun's temperature reaches as high as 27 million degrees Fahrenheit. Its rays travel 93 million miles to Earth in only eight minutes. Although we depend upon these rays for warmth, light, food, and energy, we cannot look directly upon their brilliant and powerful source.

As incredible as this nearest star seems to us, the power of the sun is infinitesimal compared to the infinite power of God. For our sun is neither the biggest nor the brightest star in the galaxy, and it—as well as untold billions of other stars—was called into existence by a mere word from God. Such power is incomprehensible to us, and yet this very power is available to us as children of God. You might want to think about accessing God's unfailing power.

A Moment to Reflect

I can do all things through Him who strengthens me.

Philippians 4:13 NASB

On what power source do you rely? Do you rely on your own power? Or do you depend on an employer, a spouse, or some other relationship to be your source of strength? Just as an electrical power source can become ineffective during a storm, human power sources sometimes become ineffective during the storms of life. People become tired, and people become weak.

God offers to be your unfailing power source. Since God is powerful enough to call the mighty sun into existence, surely he is capable of handling the details of your life. Tell him about the situations that have recently overwhelmed you. Give him the opportunity to work powerfully on your behalf today.

I sing the mighty power of God,
that made the mountains rise;
That spread the flowing seas abroad,
and built the lofty skies.
There's not a plant or flower below,
but makes Thy glories known;
And clouds arise, and tempests blow,
by order from Thy throne.
While all that borrows life from
Thee is ever in Thy care,
And everywhere that man can be,
Thou, God, art present there.

Isaac Watts

A Moment to Refresh

When a man has no strength, if he leans on God, he becomes powerful.

Dwight L. Moody

The same power that brought Christ back from the dead is operative within those who are Christ's.

Leon Lamb Morris

How great is our Lord! His power is absolute! His understanding is beyond comprehension! The LORD supports the humble, but he brings the wicked down into the dust. Sing out your thanks to the LORD; sing praises to our God with a harp. He covers the heavens with clouds, provides rain for the earth, and makes the grass grow in mountain pastures. He gives food to the wild animals and feeds the young ravens when they cry.

Psalm 147:5–9 NLT

"Not by might nor by power, but by my Spirit," says the LORD Almighty.

Zechariah 4:6 NIV

It is he [God] who made the earth by his power, who established the world by his wisdom, and by his understanding stretched out the heavens. When he utters his voice, there is a tumult of waters in the heavens, and he makes the mist rise from the ends of the earth. He makes lightning for the rain, and he brings forth the wind from his storehouses.

Jeremiah 10:12–13 ESV

POSSIBILITIES

A Moment to Rest

Most mothers have spent a good deal of time on numerous playgrounds. But do you remember your own experiences at play? Do you recall when playgrounds were places of marvel, filled with the laughter of children in their merriment? Can you recall digging gleefully in a sandbox, hoping to discover a wonderful treasure? Does the memory return of a swing that seemed to sprout wings and take you soaring above the clouds? As a child, you enjoyed the world of fascination the playground provided. A place where anything seemed possible. Yet the adult world called you to leave the playground, and increasingly life began to reveal many seeming impossibilities. Today's good news, however, is that God does not recognize anything as impossible, for he is a God of possibilities.

> *Though we stumble, we shall not fall . . . for the LORD holds us by the hand.*
>
> Psalm 37:24 NRSV

The Bible clearly illustrates that God thrills to do things that seem impossible to humans. Scripture tells of his giving sight to the blind and strength to the lame, raising people from the dead, causing barren women to bear children, healing the hopelessly diseased, parting raging rivers, defeating mighty armies, and bringing down the walls of heavily fortified cities.

Yet these instances have one characteristic in common—before a miracle occurred, somebody took God at his word. Somebody refused to acknowledge the impossible. Somebody had faith that with God, the impossible would be possible.

A Moment to Reflect

*Ah Lord GOD! Behold, You have made the heavens and the
earth by Your great power and by Your outstretched arm!
Nothing is too difficult for You, who shows lovingkindness
to thousands. . . . O great and mighty God. The LORD of
hosts is His name; great in counsel and mighty in deed.*

Jeremiah 32:17–19 NASB

Accepting a situation as impossible is always easier than
believing in a miraculous possibility, because accepting the
impossible requires nothing from you, while believing in
the possible requires faith. Those who accept the impossible
have no enemy. Those who believe in the possible must be
willing to battle doubt and fear, lies and discouragement,
critics and naysayers.

Are there situations in your life that seem hopeless? Have
you given God any chance to work in ways you cannot work,
any chance to do things you cannot do? Recognize that literally nothing is impossible with God. Claim that truth for
your life. Choose to believe God for something you cannot
accomplish on your own.

Doubt sees the obstacles, Faith sees the way;
Doubt sees the blackest night, Faith sees the day;
Doubt dreads to take a step, Faith soars on high;
Doubt questions, "Who believes?" Faith answers, "I!"

Author Unknown

Jesus replied, "What is impossible
with men is possible with God."

Luke 18:27 NIV

*I know that the LORD is great
And that our Lord is above all gods.
Whatever the LORD pleases, He does,
In heaven and in earth, in the seas
and in all deeps.*

Psalm 135:5–6 NASB

*[Jesus said,] "Everything is possible
for him who believes."*

Mark 9:23 NIV

*People may plan all kinds of things, but the
LORD's will is going to be done.*

Proverbs 19:21 GNT

*[Jesus] saw a fig tree by the side of the road
and went to it, but found nothing on it except
leaves. So he said to the tree, "You will never
again bear fruit!" At once the fig tree dried up.
The disciples saw this and were astounded.
"How did the fig tree dry up so quickly?" they
asked. Jesus answered, "I assure you that if
you believe and do not doubt, you will be able to
do what I have done to this fig tree. And not
only this, but you will even be able to say to
this hill, 'Get up and throw yourself in the sea,'
and it will. If you believe, you will receive
whatever you ask for in prayer."*

Matthew 21:19–22 GNT

*Faith does not
operate in the
realm of the possi-
ble. There is no
glory for God in
that which is
humanly possible.
Faith begins where
man's power ends.*

George Müller

*Faith sees the
invisible, believes
the unbelievable,
and receives the
impossible.*

Corrie ten Boom

OBEDIENCE OR INDEPENDENCE?

A Moment to Rest

Treat yourself to a few minutes of quiet reflection today. Consider what part obedience plays in your relationships and what the various benefits of obedience are within each one. For instance, you are in relationship with other members of society. When you obey society's laws, you enjoy the benefit of freedom and all its privileges. If you are employed, your obedience to company guidelines results in a salary and perhaps even a promotion or raise.

All heaven is waiting to help those who will discover the will of God and do it.

J. Robert Ashcroft

As a parent, you know your obedient child merits increased responsibilities and privileges. And not only that, an obedient child makes your heart glad and gives you great comfort. After all, your rules and instructions are established for the good of your children. Likewise, when you are in relationship with God, he asks for your obedience, and that obedience brings many rewards.

Sometimes, however, the idea that God desires obedience may cause your independent spirit to bristle. You may feel God is relegating you to a demeaning position. Yet the incredible truth is that obedience elevates you to be a fellow worker with God. By desiring to know and do the will of God, you actually link yourself to the whole of God's plan and purpose.

As a participator in God's work, you receive added benefits as well. Just a few that Scripture names are answered prayer, long life on earth, eternal life in heaven, God's blessing, and God's protection.

A Moment to Reflect

*Your word is a lamp to guide my feet
and a light for my path.*

Psalm 119:105 NLT

What a blessing it is that God did not leave you on your own to make moral decisions, to experiment with right and wrong and reap the harmful results of errors and miscalculations. The God who thoroughly understands the universe— because he made it—and who thoroughly comprehends eternity—because he inhabits it—this very God loved you enough to tell you what is good, what is true, what is profitable, and what is right. And not only that, he gives you *his* strength to do what is right.

Recognize that a true spirit of obedience is the result not of force but of merely a loving heart's consent. God must have a spirit in tune with his own purposes. Will your response of love be obedience?

If two angels were to receive at the same moment a commission from God, one to go down and rule earth's grandest empire, the other to go and sweep the streets of its meanest village, it would be a matter of entire indifference to each which service fell to his lot, the post of ruler or the post of scavenger; for the joy of the angels lies only in obedience to God's will.

John Newton

Does the LORD delight in burnt offerings and sacrifices as much as in obeying the voice of the LORD? To obey is better than sacrifice, and to heed is better than the fat of rams.

1 Samuel 15:22 NIV

A Moment to Refresh

The strength and happiness of a man is finding out the way in which God is going, and going that way too.

Henry Ward Beecher

By obeying Christ's commands, you will gain more than you can give.

Thomas Brooks

Jesus said to his disciples: If you love me, you will do as I command. Then I will ask the Father to send you the Holy Spirit who will help you and always be with you. The Spirit will show you what is true. The people of this world cannot accept the Spirit, because they don't see or know him. But you know the Spirit, who is with you and will keep on living in you.

John 14:15–17 CEV

Be doers of the word, and not hearers only, deceiving yourselves. . . . He who looks into the perfect law of liberty and continues in it, and is not a forgetful hearer but a doer of the work, this one will be blessed in what he does.

James 1:22, 25 NKJV

Our Father in heaven, hallowed be your name. Your kingdom come. Your will be done, on earth as it is in heaven.

Matthew 6:9–10 NRSV

Although [Jesus] was a Son, He learned obedience from the things which He suffered. And having been made perfect, He became to all those who obey Him the source of eternal salvation.

Hebrews 5:8–9 NASB

THE POWER OF MEMORY

A Moment to Rest

Pause for a few moments and recall your favorite times spent with family. Look back through the pages of an old family photo album or your child's baby book and enjoy the memories and the powerful feelings of love, joy, and security they bring. Perhaps these feelings demonstrate why God encourages his children to recall past encounters with him. God realizes you possess a memory of the spirit, and your memory has the power to influence your todays as well as your tomorrows.

Memory is a way of holding on to the things you love, the things you are, the things you never want to lose.

From the TV show *The Wonder Years*

Memory has the power to dispel fear and impart peace. When you remember God's past dealings with you—the deliverances he provided, the promises he fulfilled, the unexpected joys he freely gave—you cannot be easily haunted by fear. The past becomes a prophet of the future and assures you that God's delivering power, his faithfulness, and his loving-kindness remain forever the same.

Memory also has the power to establish your confidence. Memories of God's faithfulness give you a confidence based not in hope alone, but also in fact. Keeping memories of God close to your heart enables you to take each next step of life's journey with greater assurance.

A Moment to Reflect

The LORD's lovingkindnesses indeed never cease,
For His compassions never fail.
They are new every morning;
Great is Your faithfulness.

Lamentations 3:22–23 NASB

One purpose of the Bible is to serve as a book of remembrance. Notice how often God told his people to remember and Jesus told his disciples to remember. Memories of spiritual heritage provide encouragement and strength, so turn often to God's Word for examples of his faithfulness.

Just as you gather photos and other tokens to help you remember family events, collect memories of God's power in your life. Keep a journal of special times with God or powerful and unexpected answers to your prayers. You may want to mark favorite verses of Scripture in your Bible. Any moment when God is near is a moment you can treasure and reflect upon when you are discouraged or afraid.

The way to enrich life is to keep a retentive memory in the heart.
Look over a period of twenty years, and see the all-
covering and ever-shining mercy of God! We should lay up some
memory of the Divine triumphs which have gladdened
our lives, and fall back upon it for inspiration
and courage in the dark and cloudy day.

Joseph Parker

I remember the days of long ago; I meditate on all your
works and consider what your hands have done.

Psalm 143:5 NIV

Trust the LORD and his mighty power. Worship him always. Remember his miracles and all his wonders and his fair decisions.

1 Chronicles 16:11–12 CEV

He took a piece of bread, gave thanks to God, broke it, and gave it to them, saying, "This is my body, which is given for you. Do this in memory of me."

Luke 22:19 GNT

When you hold close your memories with God, the power of circumstance is nullified.

Melinda Mahand

I will remember the deeds of the LORD; yes, I will remember your miracles of long ago. I will meditate on all your works and consider all your mighty deeds. Your ways, O God, are holy. What god is so great as our God? You are the God who performs miracles; you display your power among the peoples.

Psalm 77:11–14 NIV

To live is to remember and to remember is to live.

Samuel Butler

[Jesus said,] "The Helper, the Holy Spirit, whom the Father will send in My name, He will teach you all things, and bring to your remembrance all things that I said to you. Peace I leave with you, My peace I give to you; not as the world gives do I give to you. Let not your heart be troubled, neither let it be afraid."

John 14:26–27 NKJV

COLOR YOUR WORLD

A Moment to Rest

As if the blue of the sky and the rich colors of the landscape were not enough, God fashioned the rainbow. It is perhaps the most incredible artistic masterpiece ever rendered. God has given you all the colors of the rainbow as well—color to transform the world, inspire your senses, and refresh you.

Every artist dips his brush in his own soul, and paints his own nature into his pictures.

Henry Ward Beecher

Even if your people look like stickmen and your horses look like . . . well, not like horses, you can still enjoy creating your own colorful artwork. Find a sheet of paper and crayons, colored pencils, watercolors, markers, anything that will give you the freedom you need. Then lose yourself in the exuberant world of blues and greens, reds and yellows, pinks and purples. Forget about traditional color combinations and experiment with your own. Your picture can be a rendering of something that has snagged your interest or a free-form collection of colorful splashes and streaks. You can even share this activity with your children. They'll be delighted to spend time making colorful creations with you.

As you work, put your heart into it, letting your eyes absorb the brilliance of the shades and tones until you can feel yourself relaxing with the wonder of art. Your adventure in art may not belong on the wall of a museum, but chances are it will look right at home on the refrigerator.

A Moment to Reflect

*Your eyes will see the king in his beauty and
view a land that stretches afar.*

Isaiah 33:17 NIV

Sometimes your inner being needs rest, and sometimes it
needs stimulation to stay healthy. Engaging in colorful, artistic exercises is like opening the drapes and letting the sun
shine through a spotless window. If you need new creative
inspiration, take some time to visit an art museum, or pick up
an art book or photo book. Enjoy the range of color, the mul-
tiplicity of form and design, the variety of expressions, perspectives, renderings.

Let the selections you see inspire your own creative endeavors.
Art nourishes your inner being—in its appreciation as much
as in its creation. If you could use a splash of color, enjoy the
creative works of others. Remember to thank God for all his
creation as well.

*The world's great canvas is offered up through the myriad
expressions of our eyes. Speak and our words weave worlds
divine as a brushstroke reveals mountains and
skies of which we have never dreamed.*

*Sing and the strains fill our souls with the magic of light
and color and shapes and movement as yet
unimagined by our minds.*

*Bow and our praise adorns the tabernacle of God,
lifting our souls to heavenly heights from
which we will descend only when we must.*

Tara Afriat

A Moment to Refresh

All great art is the expression of man's delight in God's work, not his own.

John Ruskin

A man should hear a little music, read a little poetry, and see a fine picture every day of his life, in order that worldly cares may not obliterate the sense of the beautiful which God has implanted in the human soul.

Johann Wolfgang Von Goethe

The LORD gave this message to Ezekiel. . . . All around him was a glowing halo, like a rainbow shining in the clouds on a rainy day. This is what the glory of the LORD looked like to me.

Ezekiel 1:3, 28 NLT

[God said to Noah,] "Whenever I bring clouds over the earth and the rainbow appears in the clouds, I will remember my covenant between me and you and all living creatures of every kind. Never again will the waters become a flood to destroy all life."

Genesis 9:14–15 NIV

Lift up your eyes on high,
And see who has created these things,
Who brings out their host by number;
He calls them all by name,
By the greatness of His might
And the strength of His power;
Not one is missing.

Isaiah 40:26 NKJV

The Mighty One, God, the LORD, has spoken,
And summoned the earth from the rising of the sun to its setting.
Out of Zion, the perfection of beauty,
God has shone forth.

Psalm 50:1–2 NASB

SEARCHING FOR TRUTH

A Moment to Rest

Search for a time and place to be alone with God for a while. Once you are comfortably settled, think about how much time each day you spend simply searching. How often do you search for a phone number, your child's misplaced toy, your car in a parking lot, or some item in the recesses of the refrigerator? While in the process of these searches, you are totally preoccupied with the endeavor. You think of nothing else. Yet throughout life, people are continually on a far more important search that often takes place on a subconscious level. This search is the search for truth.

> *I have chosen the way of truth; I have set my heart on your laws. . . . I run in the path of your commands, for you have set my heart free.*
>
> Psalm 119:30, 32
> NIV

Truth is not as elusive as we sometimes think. Consider, for example, that a gemologist learns to recognize a true diamond by studying the traits of a true diamond. In this way the gemologist becomes familiar with what is true. This familiarity with truth allows the gemologist to recognize any deception, any falsehood, anything less than a true gem.

So it is with truth. One does not discover truth by examining every falsehood. One learns to recognize truth by examining truth, and the place to begin discovering truth is in the person of Jesus, who plainly stated, "I am the way, the truth, and the life" (John 14:6 NKJV). What an astounding thing to say. What promise these simple words contain for all who are searching.

A Moment to Reflect

*The law was given through Moses; grace
and truth came through Jesus Christ.*

John 1:17 NIV

Some people search for truth within the realms of education, science, philosophy, or mystical spiritual practices. The best these disciplines can offer is abstract concepts and hypotheses about truth, for truth is not found within a particular discipline. Truth—just like all our other deepest needs—is found in relationship with Jesus Christ.

In Jesus, you have been given a living example of truth. He lived and walked the earth so we might have a better idea of who God is and what he is like. Jesus told one of his disciples who wanted to know more about God, "Anyone who has seen me has seen the Father!" (John 14:9 NLT). Jesus' principles and ways are true. His love is true, and his message is true.

If your heart longs for truth today, spend some time reading the Bible, God's book of truth.

Nothing will stand but truth; truth will stand when all things fail. It lives in the open air all the days of the year; it can go out at midnight as safely as at midday; it speaks to a king, to a child, to a peasant, with all the simplicity of innocence and the beauteousness of a high and noble and valiant courage.

Joseph Parker

The LORD is the true God; He is the living God and the everlasting King.

Jeremiah 10:10 NASB

A Moment to Refresh

*Jesus said to the people who believed in him,
"You are truly my disciples if you remain
faithful to my teachings. And you will know
the truth, and the truth will set you free."*

John 8:31–32 NLT

*All your words are true; all your righteous laws
are eternal. . . . I hate and abhor falsehood but
I love your law. Seven times a day I praise you
for your righteous laws. Great peace have
they who love your law, and nothing
can make them stumble.*

Psalm 119:160, 163–165 NIV

*Do not let kindness and truth leave you;
Bind them around your neck,
Write them on the tablet of your heart.
So you will find favor and good repute
In the sight of God and man.*

Proverbs 3:3–4 NASB

*When you heard the true teaching — the Good
News about your salvation — you believed in
Christ. And in Christ, God put his special
mark of ownership on you by giving you the
Holy Spirit that he had promised.*

Ephesians 1:13 NCV

*What God's Son
has told me, take
for true I do;
Truth himself
speaks truly
or there's
nothing true.*

Thomas Aquinas

*The desire for
truth is the
desire for God.*

John Macquarrie

QUIET MOMENTS FOR A MOTHER'S HEART ——— 117

WISDOM . . . NO SECRET

A Moment to Rest

Do you enjoy secrets? Recall for a moment that special feeling of delight you experienced the last time someone shared a secret surprise with you. Or what about the last time you planned a surprise for your spouse or child?

> *Wisdom is better than rubies; and all the things that may be desired are not to be compared to it.*
>
> Proverbs 8:11
> KJV

God has shared a great secret for us to find. Tucked away within the pages of Scripture lies the surprising revelation that the most valuable possession on Earth is not gold, silver, or rubies, not honor, strength, or power. Rather, the most valuable possession is the unassuming quality of wisdom.

Wisdom's value is no more a secret than any other of God's truths. The declarations regarding wisdom are contained within God's Word for all to read. This one truth is rarely taken at face value.

Perhaps part of the hesitation is that wisdom is believed to be a trait that people just naturally do or do not have. Once again, God has a great surprise. Wisdom is not simply a part of some people's nature. Wisdom is a trait any of God's children can acquire simply by asking. In fact, God actually wants you to ask. The Bible relates that when Solomon asked for wisdom, God was so pleased that he blessed Solomon not only with wisdom, but also with wealth and honor.

A Moment to Reflect

The fear of the LORD is the beginning of wisdom;
all those who practice it have a good understanding.
His praise endures forever.

Psalm 111:10 NRSV

How do you picture wisdom? Do you imagine a studious professor wearing glasses and chalk dust? Do you visualize a feeble old man sitting on a mountain, aloof and ineffectual? Or a silver-haired grandfatherly type in his rocker, ready to give instructions?

Begin today to change your mental image. The book of Proverbs in the Bible describes wisdom as a woman. She is powerful and strong, capable and confident, valuable and prized. She instructs, she blesses, and she protects. Certainly that image is much more effective in helping you understand wisdom's true value and inspiring you to seek it!

Today, may your first act be to ask God for wisdom. May your second act be to look for wisdom within the pages of God's Word. The book of Proverbs is a great place to start.

If you are wise you will show yourself rather as a reservoir
than a canal. For a canal spreads abroad the water it
receives, but a reservoir waits until it is filled before
overflowing, and this shares without loss to
itself its super-abundance of water.

Bernard of Clairvaux

A wise man is strong,
Yes, a man of knowledge increases strength.

Proverbs 24:5 NKJV

A Moment to Refresh

Wisdom is the ability to use knowledge so as to meet successfully the emergencies of life. Men may acquire knowledge, but wisdom is a gift direct from God.

Bob Jones

Surely the essence of wisdom is that before we begin to act at all, or attempt to please God, we should discover what it is that God has to say about the matter.

D. Martin Lloyd-Jones

Blessed is the man who finds wisdom, the man who gains understanding. . . . Long life is in [wisdom's] right hand; in her left hand are riches and honor. Her ways are pleasant ways, and all her paths are peace. She is a tree of life to those who embrace her; those who lay hold of her will be blessed.

Proverbs 3:13, 16–18 NIV

Wisdom is as good as an inheritance, an advantage to those who see the sun. For the protection of wisdom is like the protection of money, and the advantage of knowledge is that wisdom gives life to the one who possesses it.

Ecclesiastes 7:11–12 NRSV

How much better to get wisdom than gold! And to get understanding is to be chosen rather than silver.

Proverbs 16:16 NKJV

The wisdom from above is pure first of all; it is also peaceful, gentle, and friendly; it is full of compassion and produces a harvest of good deeds; it is free from prejudice and hypocrisy.

James 3:17 GNT

THE ONE WHO IS FAITHFUL

A Moment to Rest

Treat yourself to a time of comfort for body and spirit. Curl up in your favorite cozy place and enjoy thinking of someone you love—your son, daughter, husband. Try to choose a word that describes his or her character. You will probably find it an interesting endeavor to distill your loved one's character into a single word. The Bible, however, has the unique challenge of describing the very character of God. If you considered all the descriptions that Scripture provides and tried to distill God's character into only one word, the best choice would be the word *faithful*.

> *Though men are false, God is faithful.*
>
> Matthew Henry

At first you might disagree with the choice of *faithful* and propose that the word *loving* or *powerful* or *forgiving* would be better. But without faithfulness, any other descriptions would be unreliable. They would be meaningless because they would be momentary. Faithfulness is what causes the God you know today to be the same God you will know tomorrow.

God's faithfulness is, in essence, the very foundation of his character. Without it, other descriptions are mere sentiment, susceptible to being changed by time and circumstance. Without faithfulness, the thought of eternity would be terrifying. Because God is faithful, you are secure. You can trust what he's promised. You know that he will complete what he started.

A Moment to Reflect

*The Lord is faithful, and He will
strengthen and protect you.*

2 Thessalonians 3:3 NASB

Have you found it difficult to discover faithfulness in people or in circumstances? The hard reality is that none of the outward things of life can be relied on unconditionally—not a job, not a house, not a church, and not even good friends or family. For each of these is susceptible to time and circumstance. Only an inner, personal relationship with God can bring security. He alone is unconditionally faithful.

Know today that God's love toward you, his strength in you, his protection over you, and his provision for you will never falter. Trust him though all else seems unsettled and insecure. His faithfulness will be the one thing by which you can define your life.

*Morning by morning new mercies I see; all I have needed
Thy hand hath provided—Great is Thy faithfulness,
Lord, unto me!*

Thomas O. Chisholm

*God, who has called you into fellowship with his Son Jesus
Christ our Lord, is faithful. . . . It is because of him that you
are in Christ Jesus, who has become for us wisdom from
God—that is, our righteousness, holiness and redemption.
Therefore, as it is written: "Let him who boasts
boast in the Lord."*

1 Corinthians 1:9, 30–31 NIV

A Moment to Refresh

Your love, O LORD, reaches to the heavens,
your faithfulness to the skies.
Your righteousness is like the mighty
mountains, your justice like the great deep.
O LORD, you preserve both man and beast.

Psalm 36:5–6 NIV

I saw heaven opened, and there was a white
horse! Its rider is called Faithful and True, and
in righteousness he judges and makes war. . . .
On his robe and on his thigh he has a name
inscribed, "King of kings and Lord of lords."

Revelation 19:11, 16 NRSV

Know that the LORD your God, He is God, the
faithful God who keeps covenant and mercy for
a thousand generations with those who love
Him and keep His commandments.

Deuteronomy 7:9 NKJV

O LORD, You are my God;
I will exalt You, I will give
thanks to Your name;
For You have worked wonders,
Plans formed long ago,
with perfect faithfulness.

Isaiah 25:1 NASB

In God's
faithfulness lies
eternal security.

Corrie ten Boom

Change and decay
in all around I
see; O thou, who
changest not,
abide with me.

Henry Francis Lyte

THE PROMISE OF PEACE

A Moment to Rest

In a household of busy children and hectic schedules, finding a moment of peace and quiet can be quite a challenge for most moms. With all the demands you face during the course of the day, sometimes the only place you can find peace is within the inner recesses of your spirit. Retreat to that place of inner rest as you consider the essence of true peace.

A peaceable man does more good than a learned one.

Thomas à Kempis

Sometimes people think of peace as being the absence of war, affliction, or adversity. True peace is not the absence of something, but rather the presence of something—the presence of God within you. God's inner presence enables you to walk with assurance through the ever-changing circumstances of life. Even when you are outwardly in trouble, inwardly you can possess an unfailing peace, a consistent confidence in God, his power, and his resources.

The world seems to live in a constant state of unrest, at the mercy of what is called chance or misfortune. As God's child, you can walk in peace through the midst of a storm and, therefore, cause the world to wonder. You become a living example of a spiritual dimension that overcomes the temporal. This example opens the door for you to tell others of the God whose presence promises peace.

A Moment to Reflect

The wisdom that comes from heaven is first of all pure;
then peace-loving, considerate, submissive, full of mercy
and good fruit, impartial and sincere. Peacemakers who
sow in peace raise a harvest of righteousness.

James 3:17–18 NIV

When God's peace fills your heart, you have the potential to effect peace in the world around you, to be in fact a peacemaker. Although we tend to think of a peacemaker as someone who attempts to achieve worldwide peace, you can begin today to be a peacemaker within your own household, neighborhood, place of business, church, or community.

Is there someone with a troubled spirit you can soothe? Are there friends having a disagreement you can mediate? Is there a brewing relational storm you can help calm? Keep your eyes open for such an opportunity today. For peace, even if brought only to one heart or to one home, is a great blessing.

Lord, make me an instrument of your peace. Where there is
hatred, let me sow love. Where there is injury, pardon. Where
there is discord, vision. Where there is doubt, faith. Where
there is despair, hope. Where there is darkness, light.
Where there is sadness, joy.

Francis of Assisi

Blessed are the peacemakers: for they shall be
called the children of God.

Matthew 5:9 KJV

A Moment to Refresh

Reconciliation is not weakness or cowardice. It demands courage, mobility, generosity, sometimes heroism, an overcoming of oneself rather than of one's adversary.

Paul VI

No God, no peace. Know God, know peace.

Author Unknown

How wonderful it is to see a messenger coming across the mountains, bringing good news, the news of peace!

Isaiah 52:7 GNT

The fruit of the Spirit is love, joy, peace, patience, kindness, goodness, faithfulness, gentleness, self-control; against such things there is no law.

Galatians 5:22–23 NASB

The LORD will give strength to His people; The LORD will bless His people with peace.

Psalm 29:11 NKJV

Consider the blameless, observe the upright; there is a future for the man of peace.

Psalm 37:37 NIV

The LORD bless thee, and keep thee: The LORD make his face shine upon thee, and be gracious unto thee: The LORD lift up his countenance upon thee, and give thee peace.

Numbers 6:24–26 KJV

A HEART FULL OF PRAISE

A Moment to Rest

Think about the good things that God has provided in your life today. Has he lifted your spirits through the smile of your child? A touch from your husband? A note from your mother? Has he answered your prayer? Has he sent the encouragement of a friend? Spend a few quiet moments remembering recent blessings and praising God for each one. The Bible emphasizes that God's people are to praise him. Two of the most apparent reasons are that God deserves praise and that praise pleases him. Praise is crucial to the life of a Christian for another reason as well. The fact is that praise is one of the most incredible avenues God has given for you to know him and to release his power to work on your behalf.

> *There is nothing that pleases the Lord so much as praise.*
>
> Author Unknown

Praise puts you in a position to focus on the attributes of God, his work in your life, and his goodness toward you. This position automatically gives you an intimate awareness of who God is and how much he cares for you. In turn, this knowledge of his loving care provides you with assurance and power to face the day. Finally, your acknowledgment and appreciation of God motivate him to continue his work in your life.

Praise is given to God, but the blessings come back to you. Let your heart be full of praise for him.

A Moment to Reflect

I will give thanks to You,
O Lord my God, with all my heart,
And will glorify Your name forever.
For Your lovingkindness toward me is great.

Psalm 86:12–13 NASB

Sometimes the word *praise* can be frightening. People are not exactly sure what it is or how to do it. But praise is simply adoring God and declaring back to him the truth about who he is and what he does. There are no special words to use or positions to be in. Praise is just your heart talking to God's heart about his wonderful attributes and actions.

Will you take time to praise God today? Through praise, you take your eyes off your problems and focus instead on God. There in his presence you find hope, help, and healing. For once again, praise is given to God, but the blessings come back to you.

If any one would tell you the shortest, surest way to all hap-
piness and all perfection he must tell you to make it a rule to
yourself to thank and praise God for everything that happens
to you. For it is certain that whatever seeming calamity
happens to you, if you thank and praise God for it,
you turn it into a blessing.

William Law

I will praise you, O LORD, with all my heart; I will tell of
all your wonders. I will be glad and rejoice in you;
I will sing praise to your name, O Most High.

Psalm 9:1–2 NIV

A Moment to Refresh

I will bless the LORD at all times: his praise shall continually be in my mouth. My soul shall make her boast in the LORD: the humble shall hear thereof, and be glad. O magnify the LORD with me, and let us exalt his name together.

Psalm 34:1–3 KJV

The LORD is my strength and my song; he has become my salvation. He is my God, and I will praise him, my father's God, and I will exalt him. . . . Who among the gods is like you, O LORD? Who is like you — majestic in holiness, awesome in glory, working wonders? . . . The LORD will reign for ever and ever.

Exodus 15:2, 11, 18 NIV

Both riches and honor come from You, and You rule over all, and in Your hand is power and might; and it lies in Your hand to make great and to strengthen everyone. Now therefore, our God, we thank You, and praise Your glorious name.

1 Chronicles 29:12–13 NASB

In prayer we act like men; in praise we act like angels.

Thomas Watson

There is more healing joy in five minutes of worship than there is in five nights of revelry.

A. W. Tozer

WORDS THAT RENEW

A Moment to Rest

Without doubt, the Bible is the most magnificent book ever written. Its words are filled with encouragement and inspiration. Even more than that, the Bible is a living letter from a loving God to you. If you're like most moms, time for personal reading is close to nonexistent. The last book you read was probably a children's storybook shared with your son or daughter.

I am sorry for men who do not read the Bible every day. I wonder why they deprive themselves of the strength and the pleasure.

Woodrow Wilson

If you can, find a quiet place and a readable version of the Bible. Allow yourself to move about within its pages, soaking up God's promises, gleaning God's wisdom, and learning of God's great love for you. Read each passage twice—once for your head and once for your heart. Go slowly, and allow the richness of God's Word to calm your mind and refresh your spirit. Soon you will feel the stress and fatigue of your busy day subsiding.

Try to approach your reading with a fresh mind, and try not to take the meaning of any passage for granted, not to rely only on what you already know. Scripture is so rich with meaning that you can expect new insight and new understanding with each reading. Let God speak to you in new ways.

No matter how much time you spend reading the Bible— even if it is no more than a few minutes a day—you will come away with the riches of God's life-giving words.

A Moment to Reflect

Oh, how I love your law! I meditate on it all day long. . . .
How sweet are your words to my taste, [O Lord,] sweeter
than honey to my mouth! I gain understanding from
your precepts; therefore I hate every wrong path.

Psalm 119:97, 103–104 NIV

By the end of your busy day, you may feel used up and out of resources. Your fatigue is more than just physical tiredness; it permeates your whole being. That's precisely why the Bible is such an extraordinary gift. It has been described as a deep well filled with an endless supply of cool, fresh water. Water that can revive and renew your spirit—despite the daily rigors and demands every mom faces.

The time of day you read the Bible depends on your personal preferences and needs. No matter what time you read it, the Bible is always there to invigorate, cleanse, and restore you. Find a way to spend time reading your Bible for a few minutes each day.

One of the sweet old chapters,
That always will avail,
So full of heavenly comfort,
When earthly comforts fail,
A sweet and blessed message
From God to His children dear,
So rich in precious promises,
So full of love and cheer.

Author Unknown

A Moment to Refresh

Some read the Bible to learn and some read the Bible to hear from heaven.

Andrew Murray

I have found in the Bible words for my inmost thoughts, songs for my joy, utterance for my hidden griefs and pleadings for my shame and feebleness.

Samuel Taylor Coleridge

Your words were found, and I ate them,
And Your word was to me the
joy and rejoicing of my heart;
For I am called by Your name,
O Lord God of hosts.

Jeremiah 15:16 NKJV

The law of the Lord is perfect,
converting the soul;
The testimony of the Lord is sure,
making wise the simple;
The statutes of the Lord are right,
rejoicing the heart;
The commandment of the Lord is pure,
enlightening the eyes;
The fear of the Lord is clean,
enduring forever;
The judgments of the Lord are true
and righteous altogether.
More to be desired are they than gold,
Yea, than much fine gold;
Sweeter also than honey and the honeycomb.

Psalm 19:7–10 NKJV

[Jesus answered,] "It is written, That man
shall not live by bread alone, but by
every word of God."

Luke 4:4 KJV

HOLD ON

A Moment to Rest

As a busy mom, your hands work hard and hold many things during the course of a day: from dishes to keyboards to silky little-girl hair and little-boy hands to basketballs and kittens and Band-Aids.

So treat your hands to some luxury. Squeeze lotion into a microwave-safe cup. Liquefy the lotion by heating it for five seconds in the microwave on full power. Test the temperature with your fingertip before slathering the lotion onto your hands. Let the lotion stay on your hands for a few moments before rubbing it in. Feel the warmth penetrate your muscles, and enjoy the silky result.

> *To hold on to God is to rely on the fact that God is there for me, and to live in this certainty.*
>
> Karl Barth

As you enjoy this personal pampering, think of all the items your hands have held today. You held them because you felt a need for each one. Some you needed because they are useful or helpful. Others you needed because they are comforting or encouraging. Still others you needed simply because they are precious to your heart.

Now consider God's desire that you cling to or hold on to him. What does that desire communicate? God wants you to cling to him because he desires to help you, comfort you, encourage you, and be precious to your heart. While you cannot literally hold God in your hands, you can hold him in your thoughts, in your affections, and in your priorities.

A Moment to Reflect

Because you are my help, I sing in the shadow of your wings. My soul clings to you; your right hand upholds me.

Psalm 63:7–8 NIV

Are you holding on to worry, stress, guilt, anger, or painful memories instead of holding on to God? Full hands have to let go of something before they can hold something new, and you may have to let go of some things before you can begin to hold on to God.

Release the things that block you from spending time with God, from feeling as though you can face him. When negative thoughts and feelings try to overwhelm you, refuse to accept them and instead turn to God. Visualize yourself as a child holding tight to her mother. As you cling to God, trusting in his strength, remember that his hands are never full and they hold you securely . . . always.

Abide in me says Jesus. Cling to me. Stick fast to me. Live the life of close and intimate communion with me. Get nearer to me. . . . Never let go your hold on me for a moment. Be, as it were, rooted and planted in me. Do this and I will never fail you. I will ever abide in you.

J. C. Ryle

[Jesus said,] "Remain in me, and I will remain in you. . . . Those who remain in me, and I in them, will produce much fruit. For apart from me you can do nothing."

John 15:4–5 NLT

A Moment to Refresh

I bless the LORD who gives me counsel; in the night also my heart instructs me. I have set the LORD always before me; because he is at my right hand, I shall not be shaken.

Psalm 16:7–8 ESV

Continue in him, so that when he appears we may be confident and unashamed before him at his coming.

1 John 2:28 NIV

Test everything that is said. Hold on to what is good. Stay away from every kind of evil. Now may the God of peace make you holy in every way, and may your whole spirit and soul and body be kept blameless until our Lord Jesus Christ comes again. God will make this happen, for he who calls you is faithful.

1 Thessalonians 5:21–24 NLT

[Jesus said,] "As the Father loved Me, I also have loved you; abide in My love. If you keep My commandments, you will abide in My love, just as I have kept My Father's commandments and abide in His love. These things I have spoken to you, that My joy may remain in you, and that your joy may be full."

John 15:9–11 NKJV

Scripture and prayer serve as handles for those who would cling to God.

Melinda Mahand

He who clings to any creature must of necessity fail as the creature fails. But he who cleaves abidingly to Jesus shall be made firm in Him forever.

Thomas à Kempis

STOP AND REMEMBER

A Moment to Rest

Memories are precious. Even those stored during bad times contain crystals of hope and joy, and they remind you of God's tender hand encouraging and delivering you in your time of need. Other memories remind you of good times with images you want to keep forever—a loved one's smile, your son's first tooth, your daughter's fifth birthday party, the trip you took with your best friend.

> *God gave us memory so that we might have roses in December.*
>
> James M. Barrie

Moms spend a good bit of time rushing forward to the next task, appointment, ball practice, deadline, family meal. Stop the headlong rush and take some time to remember. Try putting together a scrapbook. It can be as uncomplicated or as creative as you want it to be. With a few easy-to-find supplies, you can record and highlight the special events and simple pleasures of your family life. Immerse yourself in your memories and work with thankfulness. Let yourself move back to another place and time.

As you move along your trail of memories, whisper a word of thanksgiving to God for each person and place God has used to decorate your life. Laugh and cry, smile and sigh as you wander through. The release of your emotions will help your tension dissipate and restore to you a sense of happiness and well-being.

A Moment to Reflect

*I thought about the former days, the years of long ago; I
will remember the deeds of the LORD. . . . I will meditate on
all your works and consider all your mighty deeds. Your
ways, O God, are holy. What god is so great as our God?*

Psalm 77:5, 11–13 NIV

God in his wisdom endowed human beings with memory—
and it is a remarkable gift. From your memories, you gain a
sense of perspective, realizing that the difficult times you go
through are part of a design. And that the joyful, happy
times interweave with those more difficult experiences to
make up the fabric of your life.

Your memories allow you to keep the people you love with you
always. And they also help you to learn from your mistakes—to
see how far you've come and how much you've grown. Allow
God to show you how, by his grace, you have made a difference
and have received a bounty of gifts from his hands.

*What a strange thing is memory, and hope;
One looks backward, the other forward.
The one is of today, the other is the tomorrow.
Memory is history recorded in our brain,
memory is a painter, it paints pictures
of the past and of the day.*

Grandma Moses

*Good people are remembered long after they are gone,
but the wicked are soon forgotten.*

Proverbs 10:7 CEV

A Moment to Refresh

*The beauty of
memory is that it
still sees beauty
when beauty
has faded.*

Paul Boese

*Memory tempers
prosperity,
mitigates
adversity, controls
youth, and
delights old age.*

Author Unknown

*One generation shall praise thy works to
another, and shall declare thy mighty acts
[O Lord]. . . . They shall abundantly utter the
memory of thy great goodness, and shall
sing of thy righteousness.*

Psalm 145:4, 7 KJV

*Search for the LORD and for his
strength; continually seek him.
Remember the wonders he has performed, his
miracles, and the rulings he has given.*

Psalm 105:4–5 NLT

*I will remember the years of the right hand of
the most High. I will remember the works
of the LORD: surely I will remember
thy wonders of old.*

Psalm 77:10–11 KJV

*The righteous will be remembered forever.
He will not fear evil tidings;
His heart is steadfast, trusting in the LORD.
His heart is upheld, he will not fear.*

Psalm 112:6–8 NASB

SWEET REST

A Moment to Rest

A quick nap in the early afternoon refreshes the body and stimulates creativity. Do you remember when your kids actually took naps and you could have a few moments to yourself? Remember when grade-school teachers told their students to put their heads down on their desks for a few minutes of quiet and rest? A little nap can be good for mothers and for teachers as well.

Try closing your office door and putting your head down on your desk for a few minutes. If you're at home, curl up on the sofa or flip back in the recliner. Close your eyes and consciously relax one part of your body at a time until you drift off into the warm cocoon of sleep. Let yourself remain in the arms of slumber for ten to fifteen minutes before rousing yourself to go on with your day.

> *I found I could add nearly two hours to my working day by going to bed for an hour after luncheon.*
>
> Sir Winston Churchill

When you wake up, you will feel energized, refreshed, and renewed. Work will seem easier and more enjoyable. Ideas will come more easily. Obstacles will seem less intimidating. Worries will seem smaller. It will be easier to trust that God is, after all, in control. He has given you sweet rest—a delightful way to recharge your mind and body. Thank him for the gift of rest.

A Moment to Reflect

I will lie down and sleep in peace, for you alone,
O LORD, make me dwell in safety.

Psalm 4:8 NIV

Your body is an amazing machine, designed to run with great efficiency. In most cases, it will keep right on moving as long as you want it to, but how much better it functions when you stop for a few minutes to rest. Rest is a natural prescription for well-being and productivity.

When your hectic life leaves you feeling dull and uninspired, try a nap. If you aren't able to fall asleep, just lean back, close your eyes, and rest for a few minutes. When you feel refreshed, thank God for knowing exactly what you need and for the remarkable resilience of the body he has given you.

When, spurred by tasks unceasing or undone,
You would seek rest afar,
And cannot, though repose be rightly won—
Rest where you are.
Neglect the needless; sanctify the rest;
Move without stress or jar;
With quiet of a spirit self-possessed.
Rest where you are.

Author Unknown

[Jesus said,] "Come to Me, all you who labor and
are heavy laden, and I will give you rest."

Matthew 11:28 NKJV

On my bed I remember you; I think of you through the watches of the night. Because you are my help, I sing in the shadow of your wings.

Psalm 63:6–7 NIV

Keep sound wisdom and discretion. . . . When you lie down, you will not be afraid; When you lie down, your sleep will be sweet.

Proverbs 3:21, 24 NASB

The sleep of the working man is pleasant, whether he eats little or much.

Ecclesiastes 5:12 NASB

The LORD is my shepherd; I have everything I need. He lets me rest in fields of green grass and leads me to quiet pools of fresh water. He gives me new strength. He guides me in the right paths, as he has promised. Even if I go through the deepest darkness, I will not be afraid, LORD, for you are with me.

Psalm 23:1–4 GNT

I lie down and sleep; I wake again, because the LORD sustains me.

Psalm 3:5 NIV

Sleep recreates. The Bible indicates that sleep is not meant only for the recuperation of a man's body, but that there is a tremendous furtherance of spiritual and moral life during sleep.

Oswald Chambers

Those whose spirits are stirred by the breath of the Holy Spirit go forward even in sleep.

Brother Andrew

A POET'S HEART

A Moment to Rest

Poetry is something many moms experience only as they help their children memorize a piece for a school assignment or church program. Or in a child's book of nursery rhymes. But poetry can be a joy—even for busy mothers. A poet's words can grace the reader with beauty, laughter, romance, and much more. There is seemingly no end to the combinations of words and thoughts and emotion that poetry lays out—timeless gifts offered for your benefit.

> *Poetry is the language in which man explores his own amazement.*
>
> Christopher Fry

Find a moment to wrap yourself up in a poem. Choose several that you really like and spend a few minutes reading them, soaking up the emotions of love and joy and sorrow and triumph they provide. Read them slowly, taking in each word, tuning in to the rhythms and rhymes. Soon you'll sense them dancing along the edges of your mind, urging you to come out and play awhile, happy and carefree.

And if you begin to hear your own rhythms and rhymes during your poetry breaks, don't hesitate to exercise your own creativity. It won't be long before your inner being will be spilling over with inspiration you can apply to many other areas of your life. When this inspiration comes, roll with it; allow it to become part of you, providing a delightful outlet for all your feelings and thoughts.

A Moment to Reflect

*My victory and honor come from God alone. He is my
refuge, a rock where no enemy can reach me. O my people,
trust in him at all times. Pour out your heart
to him, for God is our refuge.*

Psalm 62:7–8 NLT

Emotions like joy, happiness, love, and courage can be so
strong that they well up within you, struggling to find an outlet of expression. Poetry is a wonderful way to vent those feelings. Somehow the rhythms and rhymes and word pictures
allow you to express yourself in new and powerful ways.

Whether you are reading poetry or writing it, open your heart
and ask God to help you communicate all that your heart
longs to say. Then let your mind and spirit revel in the beauty
and inspiration of the verse. Grab on and let it pull you along,
ushering you into a world of enchantment.

*The poet's eye, in a fine frenzy rolling, doth glance from
heaven to earth, from earth to heaven;
and as imagination bodies forth the forms of things
unknown, the poet's pen turns them to shapes, and
gives to airy nothing a local habitation and a name.*

William Shakespeare

*The LORD's unfailing love surrounds
the man who trusts in him.
Rejoice in the LORD and be glad, you righteous;
sing, all you who are upright in heart!*

Psalm 32:10–11 NIV

O Lord, open my lips,
And my mouth shall show forth Your praise.

Psalm 51:15 NKJV

Poetry is the spontaneous overflow of powerful feelings: it takes its origin from emotion recollected in tranquility.

William
Wordsworth

O sing to the LORD a new song,
For He has done wonderful things. . . .
Shout joyfully to the
LORD, all the earth;
Break forth and sing for joy and sing praises.

Psalm 98:1, 4 NASB

[Jesus taught,] "A good tree can't produce bad fruit, and a bad tree can't produce good fruit. A tree is identified by its fruit. Figs are never gathered from thornbushes, and grapes are not picked from bramble bushes. A good person produces good things from the treasury of a good heart, and an evil person produces evil things from the treasury of an evil heart. What you say flows from what is in your heart."

Luke 6:43–45 NLT

The poet speaks to all men of that other life of theirs that they have smothered and forgotten.

Dame Edith Sitwell

Beautiful words fill my mind, as I compose this song for the king. Like the pen of a good writer my tongue is ready with a poem.

Psalm 45:1 GNT

SIMPLE TRUST

A Moment to Rest

Think back to the beginning of your relationship with God. Remember the simple trust you placed in him. Recall the wonderful release of turning yourself over to the One who is able to change you, your feelings, your circumstances.

Trust is a routine element of life. When you eat at a restaurant, you trust that the food is fresh. When you slow down on the highway, you trust that the brakes on your car work. Trust in "things" comes easily. Yet trust is not so easy in relationships with people. Remember the last time you had a checkup with a new doctor? You probably had a hard time trusting the doctor because you had no prior history to prove his or her trustworthiness.

> *Trusting God does not mean you are sure of your destiny, only that you are sure of your company.*
>
> Melinda Mahand

When your children are young, they have unshakable trust that you can fix what's wrong. They turn to you when they hurt, when they don't understand, when they are frustrated. No matter what a child faces, he is convinced that Mom is the source of all help.

Amazingly, we sometimes treat God as we treat a new doctor. We have a hard time trusting him even though he has proved his trustworthiness again and again. Make a conscious effort today to approach God as your child approaches you—with the implicit trust that he is able to take care of everything.

A Moment to Reflect

Whoever trusts in the LORD shall be safe.

Proverbs 29:25 NKJV

God invites you to return to that relationship path you started when you first trusted in him. He longs for you to look to him and his Word for guidance and help on a daily basis. He wants you to turn to him as your young child turns to you—for every need and desire.

Take out a pen and piece of paper. On one side of the paper, list times in your personal past when God proved his trust-worthiness to you. On the other side, list situations you now face where you need to trust God. Talk to God about each situation. Make the conscious choice to trust him. Let him prove himself to you once more.

Trust yourself and you are
doomed to disappointment.
Trust in your friends and
they will die and leave you.
Trust your money and you may
have it taken away from you.
Trust in reputation and some
slanderous tongues will blast it.
But trust in God and you are never to
be confounded in time or in eternity.

Dwight L. Moody

The LORD is good, a refuge in times of trouble.
He cares for those who trust in him.

Nahum 1:7 NIV

Don't put your trust in human leaders; no human being can save you. When they die, they return to the dust; on that day all their plans come to an end. Happy are those who have the God of Jacob to help them and who depend on the LORD their God, the Creator of heaven, earth, and sea, and all that is in them. He always keeps his promises.

Psalm 146:3–6 GNT

Trust in the LORD with all your heart, And lean not on your own understanding; In all your ways acknowledge Him, And He shall direct your paths.

Proverbs 3:5–6 NKJV

Blessed is the man who trusts in the LORD And whose trust is the LORD. For he will be like a tree planted by the water, That extends its roots by a stream And will not fear when the heat comes; But its leaves will be green, And it will not be anxious in a year of drought Nor cease to yield fruit.

Jeremiah 17:7–8 NASB

Trust the past to God's mercy, the present to God's love, and the future to God's providence.

Augustine of Hippo

He who trusts in himself is lost. He who trusts in God can do all things.

Alphonsus Liguori

SWEET SOUNDS

A Moment to Rest

Ah, the sweet sound of music. Since the beginning, it has soothed, calmed, inspired, and lifted souls. The experience of music has an uncanny way of evoking deep emotions—joy, sadness, tenderness, courage, love, compassion. Music brings feelings to the surface and makes you feel alive and vital.

> *Music washes away from the soul the dust of everyday life.*
>
> Berthold
> Auerbach

Give yourself a treat by switching on your radio, sound system, or portable player and losing yourself for a few wonderful moments in crisp beats and rich melodies. Let the music wash over you again and again, pulling you in and touching your heart. Listen to the words. Think about them. Then hum or sing along. Let the music flood your being until you feel it nourishing you from the inside out.

Choose a style of music that connects with you on the inside. Sit back and relax while you listen, letting the sounds take you away from cares and obligations. Or get up on your feet and dance. Forget—for just a little while—that you are a responsible mom with things to do. Just close your eyes and move your arms and legs, choreographing your own unique dance. You'll soon find yourself happy and relaxed, refreshed in a whole new way. Remember to thank God for his gift of music.

A Moment to Reflect

*Come to worship him with thankful
hearts and songs of praise.*

Psalm 95:2 CEV

Music is one of God's most gracious gifts. It can help you to connect with him, to lose yourself in worship, praise, and adoration. Music can allow you to transcend your inhibitions and move to a new level of openness. For thousands of years, men and women have used music as an expression of their love for and praise to the God of the universe.

Whether you are listening to a symphony, a hymn, or pop tunes, let the music lift you and renew you. Sing your own song of praise to God for the delightful and diverse gift of music he has placed in your life. If you listen carefully, you might even hear him singing along with you.

Yes, music is the prophet's art;
Among the gifts that God hath sent,
One of the most magnificent!
It calms the agitated heart;
Temptations, evil thoughts, and all
The passions that disturb the soul,
Are quelled by its divine control,
As the evil spirit fled from Saul,
And his distemper was allayed,
When David took his harp and played.

Henry Wadsworth Longfellow

*It is good to praise the LORD and make
music to your name, O Most High.*

Psalm 92:1 NIV

A Moment to Refresh

Music is for the soul what wind is for the ship, blowing her onwards in the direction in which she is steered.

William Booth

Music exalts each joy, allays each grief. Expels diseases, softens every pain.

John Armstrong

*Moses and the Israelites sang this song to the LORD . . .
"The LORD is my strength and my song;
he has become my salvation.
He is my God, and I will praise him, my
father's God, and I will exalt him."*

Exodus 15:1–2 NIV

*From palaces of ivory
music comes to make you happy.*

Psalm 45:8 NCV

*I will sing and praise you. Wake up, my soul. . . .
I will wake up the dawn. Lord, I will praise you
among the nations; I will sing songs of praise
about you to all the nations. Your great love
reaches to the skies, your truth to the clouds.
God, you are supreme above the skies. Let
your glory be over all the earth.*

Psalm 57:7–11 NCV

*The LORD your God is living among you.
He is a mighty savior.
He will take delight in you with gladness.
With his love, he will calm all your fears.
He will rejoice over you with joyful songs.*

Zephaniah 3:17 NLT

TIME FOR TWO WHEELS

A Moment to Rest

Fast is good! But not-quite-so-fast might be even better. So before you start up the engine on your four-wheel transportation, look around the garage and see if there isn't an adventurous two-wheel alternative. If the day is nice and you have a bit of extra time, be adventurous. Take the bike.

> *We can almost smell the aroma of God's beauty in the fresh spring flowers. His breath surrounds us in the warm summer breezes.*
>
> Gale Heide

If you're thinking, "I'm a mom, a grown-up! I don't have time to ride bikes!" think again. You don't have to cycle across Nova Scotia to enjoy the thrill. The sights, the sounds, the sun on your face, the breeze moving through your hair—those are the things you notice when you ride a bike. Once or twice around the block can be a wonderful break. As you climb astride, take a deep breath. Allow yourself to focus on the motion, the up and down of your legs on the pedals, the rubber grips and cool metal of the handlebars.

Take time to glide along and to reacquaint yourself with the neighborhood. Notice the trees, the yards, the people. Pay attention to what's new and what's not. Take the opportunity to reconnect with the world you live in. Then give thanks for what you see around you—the wonder of a squirrel racing up a tree, a dog barking in a yard, children at play. Thank God for strong lungs and strong legs and two wheels to carry you along.

A Moment to Reflect

*Love the LORD your God with all your heart, with all your
soul, and with all your strength. And these words which I
command you today shall be in your heart. You shall
teach them diligently to your children, and shall talk of
them when you sit in your house, when you walk by the
way, when you lie down, and when you rise up.*

Deuteronomy 6:5–7 NKJV

Your busy lifestyle requires quick, reliable, weatherproof transportation. But, oh, what wonders you can enjoy when you pay
attention to the journey as much as to the destination.

God has created all the beauty of this world for you. Slowing
down and taking note is an amazing way to gain perspective
and give yourself a break from the drudgery of routine.
Hopping on a bike can free you—for a few precious
moments—from the mundane and reacquaint you with the
magic of fresh air and the joy of freewheeling on the way to
nowhere in particular. As you roll along, let thankfulness fill
you; praise God for his mighty works; rejoice in his love.

*As I pass quickly through my day
I never seem to look about
And see the flowers
You've laid out.
Lord, touch my heart
And help me see
The world that you have
Made for me.*

Roberta S. Cully

*Physical exercise has some value, but spiritual
exercise is valuable in every way, because
it promises life both for the present
and for the future.*

1 Timothy 4:8 GNT

*The heavens declare His righteousness,
And all the peoples see His glory. . . .
For You, LORD, are most high
above all the earth;
You are exalted far above all gods. . . .
Rejoice in the LORD, you righteous,
And give thanks at the remembrance
of His holy name.*

Psalm 97:6, 9, 12 NKJV

*Brethren, whatever is true, whatever is honor-
able, whatever is right, whatever is pure, whatever is lovely, whatever is of good repute, if there
is any excellence and if anything worthy of
praise, dwell on these things.*

Philippians 4:8 NASB

*Happy are those who find wisdom, and those
who get understanding. . . . Her ways are ways
of pleasantness, and all her paths are peace.*

Proverbs 3:13, 17 NRSV

*To travel hopefully
is a better thing
than to arrive, and
the true success
is to labor.*

Robert Louis
Stevenson

*Every one has
time if he likes.
Business runs
after nobody: peo-
ple cling to it of
their own free will
and think that to
be busy is a proof
of happiness.*

Seneca

FRIENDS

A Moment to Rest

What a blessing friendship is. The comfort of a touch, a smile, a knowing look, a familiar voice. Your friends know you, and you feel safe with them—safe to call for no reason, to speak your mind, to unload your bundle of irritations, to share a humorous moment. With a friend you have rest and comfort and acceptance.

Friendship is a sheltering tree.

Author Unknown

As a mother, you probably spend so much time taking your children to do things with their friends that you often neglect your own friendships. Close your eyes for a moment and let the faces of your friends flow through your mind. Then let yourself choose one to call or share a cup of coffee with. If you're feeling a little down, choose someone who has a knack for cheering you up. If you are feeling insecure, choose someone who is good at making you feel that you are okay.

To find the time, you may have to say no to something a child wants to do, or you may have to ask someone else to help you with the kids. Don't let the responsibilities of motherhood make you feel there's no time for your own friends. God designed us for human companionship. Enjoy a friend today.

A Moment to Reflect

*You will keep your friends if you forgive them, but you will
lose your friends if you keep talking about what they
did wrong. . . . A friend is always a friend, and
relatives are born to share our troubles.*

Proverbs 17:9, 17 CEV

God created humans with a deep longing for fellowship,
companionship, communication. This longing is what
draws us into relationship with him. So give in to your longing and open your heart to God. Listen for his whispers—
and his mighty voice. Pour out your thankfulness, worries,
fears, hopes, dreams.

God wants to be your trusted companion . . . the first one you
turn to. You can trust him never to leave you. He is always
close by, and he never sleeps nor is he ever too busy to listen.

The next time your soul longs for fellowship, call on God.
He will always answer. He's the best friend of all.

*Oh, the comfort, the inexpressible comfort of feeling safe with
a person, having neither to weigh thoughts nor measure
words, but pouring them all out, just as they are, chaff and
grain together, certain that a faithful hand will take and sift
them, keep what is worth keeping, and with a
breath of kindness blow the rest away.*

Dinah Maria Mulock Craik

*A man of too many friends comes to ruin,
But there is a friend who sticks closer than a brother.*

Proverbs 18:24 NASB

A Moment to Refresh

> *A friend is a present you give yourself.*
>
> Author Unknown

> *A true friend unbosoms freely, advises justly, assists readily, adventures boldly, takes all patiently, defends courageously, and continues a friend unchangeably.*
>
> William Penn

Two are better than one,
Because they have a good reward for their labor.
For if they fall, one will lift up his companion.

Ecclesiastes 4:9–10 NKJV

[Jesus said], "Here I am! I stand at the door and knock. If anyone hears my voice and opens the door, I will come in and eat with him, and he with me."

Revelation 3:20 NIV

God is faithful; by him you were called into the fellowship of his Son, Jesus Christ our Lord.

1 Corinthians 1:9 NRSV

There is no greater love than to lay down one's life for one's friends. You are my friends if you do what I command. I no longer call you slaves, because a master doesn't confide in his slaves. Now you are my friends, since I have told you everything the Father told me. You didn't choose me. I chose you. I appointed you to go and produce lasting fruit, so that the Father will give you whatever you ask for, using my name. This is my command: Love each other.

John 15:13–17 NLT

DESIGNER TOUCHES

A Moment to Rest

Flowers are one of God's flamboyant designer touches: grand, robust chrysanthemums; full, creamy-soft roses; happy, yellow-and-brown daisies; dazzling bluebonnets pointing to the sky. God has placed an enormous assortment of beauty across the face of the earth. And that amazing medley of colors, smells, and textures is yours to enjoy.

One day soon, as you're walking to your office building, unloading the groceries from the van, walking to the mailbox, picking the kids up from school, or doing whatever your particular routine asks of you, slow down and take a close look at what God has done. You might see a kaleidoscope of flowery grandeur. Even dandelions in the grass or stems of goldenrod by the roadside are a visual feast. And you may think winter has nothing to offer, but for the watchful eye, it affords a rich variety of evergreen shrubs with colorful berries.

> *Don't hurry, don't worry. You're only here for a short visit. So be sure to stop and smell the flowers.*
>
> Walter C. Hagen

Let your eyes soak in the beauty and each startling detail of God's flora. Run your fingers over the petals, delighting in the delicate touch. Then, take a deep breath, drawing in the fragrances. Even on gloomy days, flowers have a way of lifting your spirits, of filling you with sunshine. Remember to thank God for his artistry in creation and for the beauty of the earth.

A Moment to Reflect

Look, the winter is past, and the rains are over and gone.
The flowers are springing up, the season of singing birds
has come, and the cooing of turtledoves fills the air.
The fig trees are forming young fruit, and the
fragrant grapevines are blossoming.

Song of Solomon 2:11–13 NLT

So much is expected of you each day. No wonder you rush about with a long list of tasks to accomplish and responsibilities to take care of. That may be why God has strewn such magnificent beauty in your path—to encourage you to stop long enough to acknowledge him.

As you think about the seemingly endless numbers and varieties of plants and creatures God has made, remember that you are his child. Those same designer hands formed you and shaped you and made you who you are. You are his joy. God delights in his people. Thank him for his designer touches that are evident in you. Marvel at the remarkable scope of God's creative genius.

I remember, I remember
The roses, red and white,
The violets, and the lily-cups,
Those flowers made of light! The lilacs,
where the robin built,
And where my brother set
The laburnum on his birthday—
The tree is living yet.

Thomas Hood

[God] commanded, "Let the earth produce all
kinds of plants..."—and it was done. So the
earth produced all kinds of plants, and God
was pleased with what he saw.

Genesis 1:11–12 GNT

Even the wilderness and desert
will be glad in those days.
The wasteland will rejoice and blossom
with spring crocuses.
Yes, there will be an abundance of
flowers and singing and joy! ...
There the LORD will display his glory,
the splendor of our God.

Isaiah 35:1–2 NLT

[Jesus said,] "Consider how the lilies grow.
They do not labor or spin. Yet I tell you,
not even Solomon in all his splendor
was dressed like one of these."

Luke 12:27 NIV

As for man, his days are like grass;
As a flower of the field, so he flourishes.

Psalm 103:15 NKJV

*The flower is
the poetry of
reproduction. It
is an example
of the eternal
seductiveness
of life.*

Jean Giraudoux

*Flowers are the
sweetest things
that God ever
made, and forgot
to put a soul into.*

Henry Ward
Beecher

THE LOVE OF GOD

A Moment to Rest

Just as food provides fuel for the body, God's love provides fuel for the spirit. Not only does God's love sustain your innermost being, but it literally gives you life. Focusing your mind on the miracle of grace brings refreshment, renewal, and rest.

> *In his love he clothes us, enfolds us and embraces us; that tender love completely surrounds us, never to leave us.*
>
> Julian of Norwich

Wherever you are, whatever you're doing, focus your mind on God and meditate on the fact that he chose to love you before you even knew him. Think back to the overwhelming love you felt for your newborn child. You were so attuned to her every need—when she was hungry or tired or needing to be held. You are God's own child, and his love for you is beyond comprehension. He too is attuned to your every need. His desire is to provide for you and care for you and help you become the woman he created you to be.

Think about how extraordinary it is that he gave you a free will, endowing you with the right to receive his love without coercion. As you think about these things, bask in the warmth of God's commitment to you, his love for you, his confidence in you. As you go on with the tasks and responsibilities of your day, hold God's love close to your heart. Draw on it for courage and encouragement. Feast on it for nourishment and sustenance. Cherish it, and it will bring life and health to your spirit.

A Moment to Reflect

Your unfailing love is as high as the heavens.
Your faithfulness reaches to the clouds.
Be exalted, O God, above the highest heavens.
May your glory shine over all the earth.

Psalm 57:10–11 NLT

God's love is a life-giving force. When you open your heart to it, his love warms and feeds your spirit. And from you, that love travels outward to others. God's love is intangible, yet your whole self connects with, responds to, and shares his love intuitively and instinctively.

The God who created the universe has chosen to pour out his love on you. In his sovereignty and wisdom, he chose to do so. What greater gift could ever be given? What greater understanding could more surely restore and reenergize you? What more could you give to your child, a friend, a co-worker than the overflow of God's love?

Jesus, lover of my soul,
Let me to thy bosom fly,
While the nearer waters roll,
While the tempest still is high;
Hide me, O my Savior, hide,
Till the storm of life is past;
Safe into the haven guide
O receive my soul at last.

Charles Wesley

A Moment to Refresh

The person you are now, the person you have been, the person you will be—this person God has chosen as beloved.

William Countryman

All God can give us is his love, and this love becomes tangible—a burning of the soul—it sets us on fire to the point of forgetting ourselves.

Brother Roger

Give thanks to the LORD, for he is good. His love endures forever. . . . Give thanks to the Lord of lords:
His love endures forever. to him who alone does great wonders,
His love endures forever. who by his understanding made the heavens,
His love endures forever.

Psalm 136:1, 3–5 NIV

God loved the world so much that he gave his one and only Son, so that everyone who believes in him will not perish but have eternal life.

John 3:16 NLT

As high as the heavens are above the earth,
So great is His lovingkindness toward those who fear Him.
As far as the east is from the west,
So far has He removed our transgressions from us.
Just as a father has compassion on his children,
So the LORD has compassion on those who fear Him.

Psalm 103:11–13 NASB

LEARNING TO COUNT

A Moment to Rest

You've heard people say, "God is good—very good!" You've sung the old hymn "Count Your Blessings." But when the dishes are piled high, there are multiple loads of laundry to be done, your child has just informed you that his book report is due tomorrow (and he hasn't started writing it) . . . On those kinds of days, it's hard to remember that God is good. And the only thing you're able to count is the number of jobs still to do.

> *If you count all your assets, you always show a profit.*
>
> Robert Quillen

Step away from everything that needs to be done and take an inventory of the good things in your life. Speak each one aloud and thank God for it. Include even those things that challenge you and keep you from getting too comfortable, for they are intended for your benefit as well. When you have finished, move on to those things that provide you with hope—things like forgiveness and eternal life. Even hope itself is a good gift from God, for without it we would not have the courage or the will to become all that he intends.

So go ahead and learn to "count the blessings"—the good things. If you run out of time, just wait for the next opportunity to take a break and start again where you left off.

A Moment to Reflect

Oh, taste and see that the LORD is good;
Blessed is the man who trusts in Him!

Psalm 34:8 NKJV

No matter what is taking place in your life right now, there are always blessings to count. Try singing a hymn or a new song of praise—something to let God know you're aware of all he's done. Think about how he's provided for you, cared for you, protected you. Even when you feel you have the least to celebrate, you receive great benefit from focusing on God rather than on your circumstances.

Whatever your situation might be, do yourself a favor—start counting the good things. Soon you will feel a soothing shower of God's love filling you to overflowing, and you will realize how much you really have and how very much God has given you.

This morning light
Splashing across the hills and illuminating the sky,
So singularly beautiful, it seems a gift meant just for me.
God's simple blessing. This newborn day
Offering up an unblemished canvas, an unwritten book
So singularly unique, it seems it was made just for me.
God's simple blessing.

Tara Afriat

The LORD is good;
His mercy is everlasting,
And His truth endures to all generations.

Psalm 100:5 NKJV

Bless the LORD, O my soul;
And all that is within me,
bless His holy name!
Bless the LORD, O my soul,
And forget not all His benefits.

Psalm 103:1–2 NKJV

I will praise you forever, O God,
for what you have done.
I will trust in your good name in
the presence of your faithful people.

Psalm 52:9 NLT

I will gladly offer you a sacrifice, O LORD;
I will give you thanks because you are good.
You have rescued me from all my troubles,
and I have seen my enemies defeated.

Psalm 54:6–7 GNT

We know that God causes everything to work
together for the good of those who
love God and are called according
to his purpose for them.

Romans 8:28 NLT

Be on the lookout
for mercies. The
more we look for
them, the more of
them we will
see. . . . Better
to lose count
while naming
your blessings
than to lose your
blessings to
counting your
troubles.

Maltbie D.
Babcock

WATCHING OVER YOU

A Moment to Rest

Your eyes work hard, so offer them a soothing treat today by placing a cool cucumber slice or a damp tea bag over each lid. As you rest your eyes, meditate on the blessing of God's eyes watching over you.

Now consider the vast amount of information your eyes give you. Each day your eyes capture innumerable visual signals that tell you about the circumstances and people in your world. Your eyes help you determine whether your spouse is sick or well, hurried or relaxed. They help you discern whether a friend is happy or upset. They help you decide whether a particular situation is safe or dangerous. They tell you what your child is doing or even what he is *thinking* of doing. Your eyes help you evaluate situations, emotions, and behaviors in order to guide, encourage, strengthen, protect, and care for yourself and those around you.

> *The eyes of the LORD search the whole earth in order to strengthen those whose hearts are fully committed to him.*
>
> 2 Chronicles 16:9
> NLT

Yet your eyes have limits. They cannot go everywhere your loved ones go. They grow weary and must rest. They have not seen every detail of the past, nor can they foresee any detail of the future. Human eyes are, after all, human eyes. But God's eyes follow your every move, and he never sleeps or grows weary. He has only your best in mind. So in this quiet moment, rest in the assurance that he is always watching over you.

A Moment to Reflect

*I will instruct you and teach you in the way which you
should go; I will counsel you with My eye upon you.*

Psalm 32:8 NASB

The eyes of God have no human limits. They reach into every
corner of this universe. They pierce the past and the future.
They do not grow weary but are always awake, always watchful. Not even a sparrow can fall to the ground without God's
seeing, knowing, caring.

Recognize today that God watches for the same reasons you
watch out for those you love. God watches because he loves
his children. His eyes are on you to guide, encourage, repri-
mand, protect, comfort, strengthen, and care for you. Thank
him today for keeping you always in his watchful eye. Trust
him to see and act on your behalf in every situation.

*It is an infinite mistake to suppose that God is enthroned far
beyond the stars, in any sense which separates him from
immediate contact with ourselves. . . . This is the essential
glory of God, and the mystery of his being, that he is far
away, yet near at hand; near at hand, yet losing nothing
through familiarity; far away, yet able to come at a
moment's notice to guide, inspire, and
sanctify his trustful children.*

Joseph Parker

*The eyes of the Lord are on the righteous and
his ears are attentive to their prayer.*

1 Peter 3:12 NIV

A Moment to Refresh

Where could I go to escape from you? Where could I get away from your presence? If I went up to heaven, you would be there; if I lay down in the world of the dead, you would be there. If I flew away beyond the east or lived in the farthest place in the west, you would be there to lead me, you would be there to help me.

Psalm 139:7–10 GNT

The LORD watches over all who honor him and trust his kindness. . . . We depend on you, LORD, to help and protect us. You make our hearts glad because we trust you, the only God. Be kind and bless us! We depend on you.

Psalm 33:18–22 CEV

This is what the LORD says: "Heaven is my throne, and the earth is my footstool. Where is the house you will build for me? Where will my resting place be? Has not my hand made all these things, and so they came into being?" declares the LORD. "This is the one I esteem: he who is humble and contrite in spirit, and trembles at my word."

Isaiah 66:1–2 NIV

The eyes of the LORD are in every place, beholding the evil and the good.

Proverbs 15:3 KJV

As a Christian is never out of the reach of God's hand, so he is never out of the view of God's eye.

Thomas Brooks

I believe he sees; therefore, even when I don't see, I still believe.

Melinda Mahand

GO AHEAD AND TALK

Conversation is the cornerstone of relationship. It is the means by which one soul connects with another. But mothers often have very little time for conversation; there always seems to be somewhere to be, someone to deliver or pick up, groceries to be bought, homework to oversee, sports and church activities to attend.

Give your inner self a welcome break by talking with a neighbor over the back fence, the person packing your groceries, another mom sitting on the sidelines at basketball practice, one of your children as you travel to your next event, or your spouse at the end of the day. No need to get deep and serious. Even topics like the weather and current events can fuel interesting, upbeat conversations. The interaction is more important than the topic.

> *Do you know that conversation is one of the greatest pleasures in life? But it wants leisure.*
>
> W. Somerset Maugham

As you converse, chase away interrupting thoughts, inhibitions, or shyness. Concentrate on the person you are speaking with. Ask open questions and listen carefully to the answers. Allow yourself to respond emotionally to what you're hearing and saying. Laugh, tell jokes, show compassion. Soon you will feel yourself relaxing and gaining new perspective on life.

Don't worry about who is doing the most talking. It's fun to lose yourself in someone else's story. Not only will your moments of conversation serve to refresh your mind and spirit, but they will almost certainly do the same for the other person.

A Moment to Reflect

If we claim to have fellowship with him yet walk in the darkness, we lie and do not live by the truth. But if we walk in the light, as he is in the light, we have fellowship with one another.

1 John 1:6–7 NIV

Despite constant motion and steady activity with people all around us, moms often feel isolated and alone. We see plenty of people, but rarely do we have the chance to interact with others beyond a hurried exchange of pleasantries. God always meant for people to know, care for, and love one another. Conversation breaks down walls and creates bridges from person to person, soul to soul.

As you go through your day, tune in to the faces of those around you. Open your heart to hear what their inner selves might have to say. Then reach out and communicate with someone. You will sense your walls coming down and your heart rising up. It's a delightful way to invest your time and bring good into two lives in the process.

Talk with us, Lord, Thyself reveal,
While there o'er earth we move;
Speak to our hearts, and let us feel
The kindling of Thy love.
With Thee conversing, we forget
All time, and toil, and care;
Labor is rest, and pain is sweet,
If Thou, my God, art here.

Charles Wesley

A man that hath friends must show himself friendly.

Proverbs 18:24 KJV

[Jesus said,] "Where two or three come together in my name, there am I with them."

Matthew 18:20 NIV

[Jesus said,] "A new commandment I give to you, that you love one another; as I have loved you, that you also love one another. By this all will know that you are My disciples, if you have love for one another."

John 13:34–35 NKJV

I have much more to say to you, but I don't want to do it with paper and ink. For I hope to visit you soon and talk with you face to face. Then our joy will be complete.

2 John 1:12 NLT

The grace of the Lord Jesus Christ, and the love of God, and the fellowship of the Holy Spirit, be with you all.

2 Corinthians 13:14 NASB

Those who revered the LORD spoke with one another. The LORD took note and listened, and a book of remembrance was written before him of those who revered the LORD and thought on his name.

Malachi 3:16 NRSV

If my heart is right with God, every human being is my neighbor.

Oswald Chambers

While the spirit of neighborliness was important on the frontier because neighbors were so few, it is even more important now because our neighbors are so many.

Lady Bird Johnson

MUD PIES AND GARDENS

A Moment to Rest

Think back to when you were a girl and had the chance to make mud pies. Brown and rich, big and little. Maybe you even added some grass and twigs for extra ingredients. If you never had the chance to make your own mud pies as a child, perhaps you've made them with your own children. Mud pies aren't about eating; they are all about digging in the dirt and feeling the earth squish through your fingers. The instinct to connect with the soil has been handed down from the first gardeners—Adam and Eve.

> *God Almighty first planted a garden; and indeed, it is the purest of human pleasures.*
>
> Francis Bacon

You may not be in the mood to play in the mud today, but take a few minutes to dig a little hole and plant something. Don't panic if you don't have a green thumb. It isn't necessary to put in an entire vegetable garden or to landscape your yard. Gardening can be as simple as planting one small flower.

Once you've decided what to plant where, just dig in. Turn the soil, letting your senses take in the experience. Focus next on the wonderful fragrance. While you work, imagine God planting you in the nourishing soil of his love. Put the plant in place and pack the dirt around it. Then water the plant gently, reminding yourself of the tender way God waters your spirit.

*I delight greatly in the LORD; my soul rejoices in my
God. . . . As the soil makes the sprout come up and a
garden causes seeds to grow, so the Sovereign LORD will
make righteousness and praise spring up.*

Isaiah 61:10–11 NIV

When life seems too complicated or feels a bit overwhelming, the very exercise of manipulating the soil, planting, watering, and harvesting can help keep things in perspective. Gardening serves as a reminder that you still live in a world that is subject to the God-given cycle of life, and you will reap the fruit of your labor.

Working the soil and watching a living thing thrive and grow will help you reclaim your sense of purpose and your personal worth—reestablishing your belief that life is worth living and your dreams are attainable. Digging in the dirt is an exercise in faith, hope, and love.

*Oh, Adam was a gardener, and God who made him sees
That half a proper gardener's work is done upon his knees,
So when your work is finished,
You can wash your hands and pray
For the Glory of the Garden, that it may not pass away!*

Rudyard Kipling

*The LORD God placed the man in the Garden
of Eden to tend and watch over it.*

Genesis 2:15 NLT

A Moment to Refresh

To own a bit of ground, to scratch it with a hoe, to plant seeds, and watch their renewal of life—this is the commonest delight of the race, the most satisfactory thing a man can do.

Charles Dudley Warner

The kiss of sun for pardon, The song of the birds for mirth, One is nearer God's Heart in a garden Than anywhere else on earth.

Dorothy Gurney

God has made everything beautiful for its own time. He has planted eternity in the human heart.

Ecclesiastes 3:11 NLT

The LORD God planted a garden toward the east, in Eden; and there He placed the man whom He had formed. Out of the ground the LORD God caused to grow every tree that is pleasing to the sight and good for food.

Genesis 2:8–9 NASB

[Jesus said,] "A man scatters seed on the ground. Night and day, whether he sleeps or gets up, the seed sprouts and grows, though he does not know how. All by itself the soil produces grain—first the stalk, then the head, then the full kernel in the head."

Mark 4:26–28 NIV

Jesus said, "How can I describe the Kingdom of God? What story should I use to illustrate it? It is like a mustard seed planted in the ground. It is the smallest of all seeds, but it becomes the largest of all garden plants; it grows long branches, and birds can make nests in its shade."

Mark 4:30–32 NLT

STRETCH BODY AND SOUL

A Moment to Rest

The human body is amazing. Though it consists of little more than mass, muscle, and matter, God has created it to act and react in unison with the soul. Dancers, for example, have long understood the tenacious link between body and soul—the glory of moving one while moving the other.

You can feel the effects of moving body and soul without becoming a ballerina. It only takes a little stretching and bending. When the kids are occupied elsewhere, find a spot where you feel comfortable. It doesn't matter if that place is in the backyard, in the middle of the living room, or in the privacy of your bedroom. Slowly focus on one limb, one muscle at a time, stretching carefully just until you sense that your body is waking up and releasing its stiffness.

Better to bend than break.

Scottish Proverb

Bend from the waist and then from the side. Lift your arms above your head and stretch them as high as you can. Lock your fingers together and push up onto your tiptoes. As you move, your body will begin to release pent-up tension and stress. Add some music, then relax and move, relax and move, until your body and soul are singing together. When you're finished, take a few minutes to rest and enjoy your inner harmony.

A Moment to Reflect

Your ears will hear a word behind you, "This is the way, walk in it," whenever you turn to the right or to the left.

Isaiah 30:21 NASB

If you find it difficult to loosen up and stretch in your worldview, in your personal vision and creativity, in your interaction with others, in your parenting style . . . stretching your arms and legs and learning to twist and turn and bend may be just the right place to start.

As you reach with your arms, reach with your heart and soul as well, asking God to help you find new perspectives, new approaches, and new solutions to old problems. You might be surprised to learn how many opportunities come your way when you begin to stretch and bend with the challenges in your life.

Whenever I go running
Across the rugged ground,
My legs stretch out before me
And my heart begins to pound.
My arms pump quickly up and down
In rhythm at my side
And my spirit lifts within me
Overjoyed with the ride.
My lungs burn ever so slightly
Breathing in the morning air
And my soul vibrates with happiness
Releasing every care.

Tara Afriat

We are the temple of the living God.
As God said:
"I will live in them and walk among them.
I will be their God, and they will be my people."

2 Corinthians 6:16 NLT

Do not call to mind the former things,
Or ponder things of the past.
Behold, I will do something new,
Now it will spring forth;
Will you not be aware of it?
I will even make a roadway in the wilderness,
Rivers in the desert.

Isaiah 43:18–19 NASB

He gives power to the weak,
And to those who have no might
He increases strength.
Even the youths shall faint and be weary,
And the young men shall utterly fall,
But those who wait on the LORD
Shall renew their strength;
They shall mount up with wings like eagles,
They shall run and not be weary,
They shall walk and not faint.

Isaiah 40:29–31 NKJV

Life is not merely
being alive, but
being well.

Martial

The human body
is a machine
which winds its
own springs: the
living image of
perpetual motion.

Julien Offray
de La Mettrie

CREATURE COMFORT

A Moment to Rest

Pets may chirp, bark, meow, oink, or swim quietly. Pets bring love, loyalty, laughs, and other wonderful things to your life. They provide companionship for you and your children and spark contentment. Many of them love unconditionally, work diligently to please you, and want only to be with you.

All things bright and beautiful, All creatures great and small, All things wise and wonderful, The Lord God made them all.

Cecil Frances Alexander

If you have a pet in your life, take a few minutes from your busy day and enjoy what God has given you. Talk up a storm— pets are great listeners, and they never give away your secrets. But do more than talk. Take a little vacation into your pet's world. Lie down beside the fire with your dog, slouch on the sofa with your cat, perch on a chair near your bird's cage. Then let your pet lead the way, initiating affection and play. Making a solid connection with another living thing can be delightful. Marveling at the complexity and detail of God's creatures is humbling.

If you don't have a pet, animals can still provide a quiet moment to reenergize your inner being. Hang a bird feeder outside your window and marvel at the numbers and kinds of birds that come to eat. Visit a pond and feed the ducks and geese, or sit in the park and watch a child play with his dog. You can even take a few minutes to watch the squirrels racing around your backyard.

Let God's creatures draw your thoughts and your heart toward him.

A Moment to Reflect

My mouth will speak in praise of the LORD.
Let every creature praise his holy name for ever and ever.

Psalm 145:21 NIV

God meant for animals to enrich your life. As you spend time with your pet, allow yourself to soak up the warmth and rest in it. Take time to thank God for caring so much about you that he created more than the beauty of the mountains and the oceans and the sky. As an expression of his creative genius, he has also given you living things. Creatures to love, care for, protect.

Enjoy the living gift that God has given you. Let the birds and the fish and the beasts encourage, refresh, and comfort your spirit, just as God intended.

The wolf also shall dwell with the lamb,
The leopard shall lie down with the young goat,
The calf and the young lion and the fatling together;
And a little child shall lead them.
The cow and the bear shall graze;
Their young ones shall lie down together;
And the lion shall eat straw like the ox.
The nursing child shall play by the cobra's hole,
And the weaned child shall put his hand in the viper's den.
They shall not hurt nor destroy in all My holy mountain,
For the earth shall be full of the knowledge of the LORD.

Isaiah 11:6–9 NKJV

A Moment to Refresh

*Love the animals:
God has given
them the
rudiments of
thought and
joy untroubled.*

Fyodor
Dostoyevsky

*The great pleasure
of a dog is that
you may make a
fool of yourself
with him and not
only will he not
scold you, but he
will make a fool of
himself too.*

Samuel Butler

*Out of the ground the LORD God formed every
animal of the field and every bird of the air, and
brought them to the man to see what he would
call them; and whatever the man called every
living creature, that was its name. The man
gave names to all cattle, and to the birds of the
air, and to every animal of the field.*

Genesis 2:19–20 NRSV

*He sends forth springs in the valleys;
They flow between the mountains;
They give drink to every beast of the field;
The wild donkeys quench their thirst.
Beside them the birds of the heavens dwell;
They lift up their voices among the branches.*

Psalm 104:10–12 NASB

*Instruct those who are rich in this present world
not to be conceited or to fix their hope on the
uncertainty of riches, but on God, who richly
supplies us with all things to enjoy.*

1 Timothy 6:17 NASB

*God gave Solomon very great wisdom, discern-
ment, and breadth of understanding. . . .
He would speak of animals, and birds,
and reptiles, and fish.*

1 Kings 4:29, 33 NRSV

HEARTS FULL OF THANKFULNESS

A Moment to Rest

Day by day, week by week, people pass through your life, touching you with wisdom, encouragement, and hope. Some bring physical blessings, some give glimpses into the meaning of life, and others bring laughter and optimism.

Circumstances have a way of bringing to your mind lessons learned and gifts given by the people in your sphere of existence. Remind yourself of the people God has sent your way. Think about former teachers and professors, friends, mentors at work or church, your own children, your life partner, your parents. Then find notepaper and a pen. Before you begin to write your note of thanks, sit back and focus on the person to whom you are writing and meditate on what he or she has meant to you. Picture

> *Thanksgiving is good but thanks-living is better.*
>
> Matthew Henry

the person in your mind and allow your thoughts and emotions to carry you where they want to go. Even if you no longer know how to reach the person, or even if he or she is no longer living, writing that note can be a wonderful, soul-enriching experience.

When you're ready to write, let your feelings flow freely. Don't worry about using the right words, just speak from your heart. The very act of writing out your thank-you affirms both the giver and the receiver, and it reestablishes those special words and actions that so blessed you in the past.

A Moment to Reflect

We give thanks to you, O God; we give thanks;
your name is near. People tell of your wondrous deeds.

Psalm 75:1 NRSV

Exercising thankfulness feels like an adrenaline rush for your inner self. It's a great way to lift your spirits on a not-so-happy day or to feel the warmth of sunshine when the weather is cold and dreary. And when you acknowledge your thankfulness, God blesses again.

Thanking those whose lives have touched yours can boost your self-esteem and inspire you in your relationships with others, motivating you to pass the wisdom and encouragement and hope along. What a marvelous way to honor those who have given of themselves to you, while, at the same time, refreshing your own spirit. And as you live thankfully, your children will see and learn and begin to live in the same way—passing to the next generation the joy of living with hearts full of thankfulness and praise.

In ordinary life we hardly realize that we receive a great deal
more than we give, and that it is only with gratitude that
life becomes rich. It is very easy to overestimate
the importance of our own achievements in
comparison with what we owe others.

Dietrich Bonhoeffer

The right word at the right time is
like precious gold set in silver.

Proverbs 25:11 CEV

*Worry weighs a person down; an encouraging
word cheers a person up.*

Proverbs 12:25 NLT

*Gratitude is born
in hearts that take
time to count up
past mercies.*

Charles Edward
Jefferson

*Give thanks in all circumstances; for this is the
will of God in Christ Jesus for you.*

1 Thessalonians 5:18 NRSV

*Encourage each other and build each other up,
just as you are already doing.*

1 Thessalonians 5:11 NLT

*Thou has given so
much to me. . . .
Give me one
thing more—a
grateful heart.*

George Herbert

*I am a companion of all those who fear You,
And of those who keep Your precepts.
The earth is full of Your
lovingkindness, O LORD;
Teach me Your statutes.*

Psalm 119:63–64 NASB

*The LORD is my strength and my shield;
My heart trusted in Him, and I am helped;
Therefore my heart greatly rejoices,
And with my song I will praise Him.*

Psalm 28:7 NKJV

GOD IS READY TO LISTEN

A Moment to Rest

Slow down today to refresh your spirit by spending some one-on-one time with God. Take advantage of a break in the day—when the kids are napping, at school, or doing their own thing—to reenergize and focus on God. Take a rocker outside to your patio, jump into an outdoor swing, or take a lawn chair and sit in the middle of your garden. Enjoy the beauty of God's world as you spend some time with him today.

> *There are no depths from which the prayer of faith cannot reach heaven.*
>
> John Blanchard

Such moments are rare these days. In fact, we spend a great deal of our time and money making sure we can stay in constant touch with others who are important in our lives. We purchase everything from baby monitors to cell phones so we can stay in touch with family and friends. We leave messages on answering machines and pagers. We regularly use overnight mail and e-mail. We sometimes resort to notes hastily scrawled with pen on paper.

Each of these communication devices attempts to bring together people who are separated by time, distance, or busy schedules. Even when we use them all and use them well, we are often left with the uneasy realization that our exchanges of information consist of shallow tidbits of fact or opinion rather than of true conversation. But conversation with God can be rich and full and requires no electronic equipment. Simply an open heart.

A Moment to Reflect

Before they call, I will answer;
And while they are still speaking, I will hear.

Isaiah 65:24 NASB

Wherever you are today—whatever your need, whatever your heartache, whatever your fear—know that God is waiting to hear from you. You do not need high-tech communications systems to send your message to his ears. You can simply talk to him about the concerns that fill your heart. It truly is no more complicated than that. Just talk to him. You don't need special words; you don't have to cover a specific prayer agenda.

When you talk to God, he will hear you. At the sound of your voice, he will listen patiently, attentively, and lovingly. Pour out your heart to God as you would confide in your best friend; enjoy the comfortable companionship that comes from knowing that you are totally accepted as you are.

Never too far I've fled,
Never too softly said,
Never too choked with tears,
Never too wrapped in fears,
—My Father heard all.
Swift He ran to my side,
Heeded each anguished cry,
Brushed every tear away,
Strengthened me for the day,
—Answered my call.

Melinda Mahand

A Moment to Refresh

*More things are
wrought by prayer
than this world
dreams of.*

Alfred, Lord
Tennyson

*Groanings which
cannot be uttered
are often prayers
which cannot
be refused.*

Charles Haddon
Spurgeon

*The LORD is far from the wicked,
But He hears the prayer of the righteous.*

Proverbs 15:29 NKJV

*I [Jesus] tell you: When you pray and ask for
something, believe that you have received it, and
you will be given whatever you ask for.*

Mark 11:24 GNT

*Confess your sins to one another, and pray for
one another so that you may be healed.
The effective prayer of a righteous
man can accomplish much.
Elijah was a man with a nature like ours, and
he prayed earnestly that it would not rain,
and it did not rain on the earth for
three years and six months.
Then he prayed again, and the sky poured rain
and the earth produced its fruit.*

James 5:16–18 NASB

*In my distress I called to the LORD; I cried to
my God for help. From his temple he heard my
voice; my cry came before him, into his ears. . . .
He rescued me from my powerful enemy, from
my foes, who were too strong for me.*

Psalm 18:6, 17 NIV

THOUGHTS OF GOD

A Moment to Rest

It's easy to get caught up in the everyday routine, completely absorbed in getting everything done. Moms juggle so many responsibilities for so many people. Who has the time to see beyond the routine?

But nothing has the power to lift your spirit from this earthly realm to heavenly heights like filling your mind with thoughts of your great Creator. Part worship and part prayer, thoughts of God are reminders that you are loved and watched over. They chase fears and anxieties. They celebrate life over death, victory over defeat, joy over sorrow.

Settle back and close your eyes. Let your mind reflect on God's greatness, his power, and his majesty. Then consider a few of God's characteristics—love, joy, peace, patience, kindness, goodness, faithfulness, gentleness, self-control. Reflect on how God's love has touched your life, how his peace has touched your life, his joy, his patience, his kindness, and so forth. As these thoughts evoke emotions, don't hesitate to express them. Free the tears of thanksgiving, the smiles of joy, the sighs of peace, and let them wash over you.

As you focus on God, feel yourself soaring above the cares of the day, looking at things with a new perspective, gaining strength, and experiencing a resurgence of creativity.

> *The thought of God is never a burden; it is a gentle breeze which bears us up, a hand which supports us and raises us, a light which guides us, and a spirit which vivifies us though we do not feel its working.*
>
> Francesco
> Malaval

A Moment to Reflect

People who are ruled by their desires think only of them-
selves. Everyone who is ruled by the Holy Spirit thinks
about spiritual things. If our minds are ruled by our
desires, we will die. But if our minds are ruled
by the Spirit, we will have life and peace.

Romans 8:5–6 CEV

God's thoughts are always about his people, his children, those who trust him. When your thoughts are on him, you make a connection—a connection that heals and refreshes your spirit. If your thoughts keep you earthbound, focus them on the One who transcends the affairs of this world. If your thoughts leave you feeling mortal and unworthy, turn them to the One who has given you eternal life and made you worthy to be called his child.

God is pleased when you think about him because he knows that doing so will fill you with hope and change your life. Let your mind move beyond the moment and into his presence.

Was it hope deferred
or a dream once loved,
now lost that led me to this valley
of dark, despairing thoughts?
It is only the thought of You,
of Your gentle Spirit and unfailing love,
that guides my spirit home again upon the wings of a Dove.

Tara Afriat

Great is the LORD, and greatly to be praised,
In the city of our God, His holy mountain.
Beautiful in elevation, the joy of
the whole earth.

Psalm 48:1–2 NASB

When I remember You on my bed,
I meditate on You in the night watches.
Because You have been my help,
Therefore in the shadow of Your
wings I will rejoice.

Psalm 63:6–7 NKJV

I will extol You, my God, O King;
And I will bless Your name forever and ever.
Every day I will bless You,
And I will praise Your name forever and ever.
Great is the LORD, and greatly to be praised;
And His greatness is unsearchable.

Psalm 145:1–3 NKJV

Whatever is true, whatever is noble, whatever is
right, whatever is pure, whatever is lovely,
whatever is admirable — if anything is excellent
or praiseworthy — think about such things.

Philippians 4:8 NIV

Without doubt, the mightiest thought the mind can entertain is the thought of God, and the weightiest word in any language is its word for God.

A. W. Tozer

The Father of all . . . is all understanding, all spirit, all thought, all hearing, all seeing, all light, and the whole source of every-thing good.

Irenaeus

From the day I was born,
I have been in your care,
and from the time of my birth,
you have been my God.

Psalm 22:10 CEV

*Can a mother forget
her nursing child?
Can she feel no love for
the child she has borne?
But even if that were possible,
I would not forget you!
See, I have written your name
on the palms of my hands.*

Isaiah 49:15–16 NLT